If You Know Not Me, You Know Nobody

Part I and Part II

Thomas Heywood

Contents

INTRODUCTION.

The two plays, or one play in two parts, here reprinted, were extremely popular in their day, and went through various editions. Both had the general title, "If You know not Me, You know Nobody;" and the first part had the sub-title of "The Troubles of Queen Elizabeth," and the second part, the sub-title, (if such it may be called) "With the Building of the Royal Exchange, and the famous Victory of Queen Elizabeth in the year 1588;" those events forming most prominent incidents. The first part was originally published in 1605, and reprinted in 1606, 1608, 1613, and 1632: the second part was originally published in 1606, and reprinted in 1609, 1623, and 1633, all the editions being in 4to.

For the use of most of these, and especially of the earliest and rarest impressions, our Society has once more been under obligations to the Duke of Devonshire. The edition of the second part, in 1609, although it does not differ materially from others, is, we believe, unique in his Grace's library. The British Museum has no perfect copy of the earliest impressions.

The first part, (which we may call " The Troubles of Queen Elizabeth ") as it has come down to us, can only be considered the fragment of a play; and, upon evidence we shall adduce presently, we may assume that it found its way to the press by means of short-hand notes, taken in the theatre while the drama was in a course of representation. Why the author did not think it worth while, in any subsequent impression, to render it more complete, we know not. The second part, which deals with the events of Elizabeth's reign, as our readers will perceive, is much more perfect, and runs out to a much greater length: from that, we feel persuaded, nothing important was omitted. When, therefore, Heywood printed, in his " Pleasant Dialogues and Dramas, 8vo, 1637, (p. 248) the following Prologue and Epilogue, he must have intended them, and the introduction to them, to apply only to the first part, " The Troubles of Queen Elizabeth," beginning "in her minority," and ending with her accession to " the royal throne, a potent Queen," in November, 1558.

" *A Prologue to the Play of Queen Elizabeth, as it was last revived at the Cockpit, in which the Author taxeth the most corrupted copy now imprinted, which was published without his consent.*

" PROLOGUE.

" Plays have a fate in their conception lent;
Some so short liv'd, no sooner show'd than spent,
But born to-day, to-morrow buried, and
Though taught to speak, neither to go nor stand.
This, (by what fate I know not) sure no merit,
That it disclaims, may for the age inherit,
Writing 'bove one and twenty; but ill nurst,
And yet receiv'd, as well perform'd, at first,

Grac'd and frequented for the cradle age,
Did throng the seats, the boxes, and the stage;
So much, that some by Stenography drew
The plot, put it in print, (scarce one word true)
And in that lameness it hath limp'd so long,
The Author now, to vindicate that wrong,
Hath took the pains upright upon its feet
To teach it walk: so please you, sit and see't.

" EPILOGUE.

" The Princess, young Elizabeth, y' have seen
In her minority, and since a Queen;
A subject, and a sovereign: in the one
A pitied Lady; in the royal throne
A potent Queen. It now in you doth rest
To know in which she hath demean'd her best."

The Cockpit Theatre was in Drury Lane; but at what precise date the "Play of Queen Elizabeth" (meaning, as we apprehend, the first part, or "The Troubles of Queen Elizabeth") had been revived there, we have no means of ascertaining; but, were we to make a guess upon the point, we should say that it occurred not long before 1632, when the last of the old editions came from the press. The renewed popularity of the drama, with Heywood's help to set it "upright upon its feet," may have induced the bookseller to speculate upon selling a sufficient number to reward his pains; and, as he could obtain no more complete manuscript from the playhouse, he was obliged to content himself with reprinting " the most corrupted copy," which the author about five years afterwards condemned, explaining, at the same time, how it had been surreptitiously procured.

The second part, (the history of the reign of Eliza-

beth) as we have stated, is not at all in the same pre-
dicament. We probably have it in the editions of 1606,
1609, and 1623, pretty much in the form in which it
came from Heywood's pen, when it was first acted,
quite early in the reign of James I. In the edition of
1633 we find it most materially altered subsequent
to the " Chorus " (on p. 151 of our reprint); and
the " Chorus " itself is there new, having been de-
signed to prepare the spectators for the great event
about to succeed in the representation, viz., the defeat
of the Spanish Armada. This incident had been but
briefly and imperfectly treated in previous editions,
and it seems more than likely that Heywood himself
introduced the changes, and made the additions, on
revival, for the sake of giving the drama increased
effect and greater novelty. That revival, we take
it, followed the revival of the first part of the same
subject, and was perhaps consequent upon the favour
with which the renewed performance of the first part
had been received by public audiences at the Cockpit
Theatre.

Our impression of this portion of the drama
(we mean the portion including and following the
" Chorus") is from the edition of 1633, under the
persuasion that the author meant that his work should
permanently (as far as such productions were at that
period considered permanent) bear that shape. However, for greater completeness, and to afford ready
means of comparison, we have subjoined to the present Introduction the brief scenes of this conclusion
of the drama, as they appear in the impressions of

1606, 1609, and 1623. Thus the Members of our Society will have before them this play as Heywood first wrote it, and as we may believe he subsequently altered it. The fulness and entireness of the second part of the whole drama on the story of Queen Elizabeth is in strong contrast with the meagre incompleteness of the first part.

The two parts of " Edward IV.," and the two parts of " Elizabeth," are the only plays strictly founded upon English history that Thomas Heywood has left behind him. The first have been long in the hands of our Members; and it will be now seen, that in the last the author has proceeded upon the same plan, not adhering to minute facts, nor to exact dates, farther than suited his purpose as a dramatic poet. In this respect, he only followed the example which had been set him by Shakespeare, and from which those, who of old adopted similar subjects as the foundations of their dramas, did not deviate. They allowed the imaginations of their auditors the freest, fullest, and widest range, and relied upon the exercise of those imaginations to reconcile, not merely improbabilities, but often impossibilities, in reference to time, place, and action. In point of character, as regarded the persons of their dramas, they were wonderfully consistent; but their chief aim was to compose a play that would attract by the novelty of its subject, and gratify by the variety of its incidents.

Besides the first part of " If You know not Me, You know Nobody," which is devoted to the " Troubles of Queen Elizabeth," Heywood left behind him a prose narrative of the events of her life, from the elevation of her sister to her own accession. In this history he goes over many of the circumstances of his play; and it is the more worthy of attention, because it may be said in a degree to supply some of the obvious deficiencies of his drama, in the curtailed and decrepit shape in which it has reached our hands. Of this work little or no notice has been any where taken; and it will be our business on the present occasion to supply such extracts from it, as afford illustrations of the scenes of the drama which comes first in the following sheets. It was printed in London, under the subsequent title:—

"England's Elizabeth: her Life and Troubles, during her Minoritie from the Cradle to the Crowne. Historically laid open and interwoven with such eminent Passages of State as happened under the Reigne of Henry the Eight, Edward the Sixt, Q. Mary; all of them aptly introducing to the present Relation. By Tho. Heywood.—London, printed by John Beale, for Philip Waterhouse, and are to be sold at his Shop at St. Paul's head, neere London-stone. 1631."

This is a small 8vo, or 12mo, of 234 pages, besides the preliminary matter, that deserves attention from one singular circumstance that has hitherto entirely escaped remark. It is that, after the dedication to Lord Hunsdon, subscribed "Tho. Heywood," comes an Epistle to the Reader, to which the initials N. R. are appended, and which must, in fact, have belonged to some other production upon the same subject, and that production a poem. N. R. (whoever he may have been) says, "I doubt not but that they will spare this argument for the worth thereof; and though their carping may correct my *Poeme*, yet they will

have a reverent respect of the person here drawne
out."

N. R. could not be Thomas Heywood; and his prose
" relation " of the early events of the life of Elizabeth could not be called, nor considered a " Poem."
N. R. proceeds to add a passage, which we extract
partly for its own sake, but principally because it
relates to an individual who contributed some well
known lines upon Shakespeare prefixed to the first
folio of his plays—Hugh Holland.

" As for those passages (says N. R.) in the character of King Edward
the Sixth, and the Lady Jane Gray and others—*vix ea nostra voco*.　I
have borrowed them from my good friend, Mr. H. H., Stationer; who
hath not only conversed with the titles of bookes, but hath looked into
them, and from thence drawn out that industrious Collection intituled
Herologia Anglicana."

Another circumstance deserves observation, in reference to Heywood's " England's Elizabeth," before
we proceed to quote from it.　We allude to the fact
that, so popular was the work immediately after
its appearance in London in 1631, it was in the
very next year reprinted in Cambridge.　It was not
merely a new title-page, with " Cambridge" and the
date of 1632 upon it, prefixed to some unsold copies,
but it was entirely a new impression, from different
types, although for the same bookseller, who perhaps
had a shop also in the University.　This edition is
likewise incidentally connected with our great drama-
tist; since the frontispiece, a portrait of Elizabeth, and
a work of great delicacy, is by the same artist—
Martin Droeshout—who engraved the head of Shakespeare on the title-page of the folio of 1623.　This

Cambridge impression of Heywood's "England's Elizabeth" has not any where been mentioned, and we do not recollect to have seen the full length of the Queen enumerated among the productions of Droeshout's graver.[1]

We now proceed to make some important extracts from Heywood's prose narrative, introducing each quotation by a reference to the passage to which it relates in his play.

PAGE 8.

"*Enter* TAME *and* CHANDOS, *with Soldiers, drum, &c.*

"*Tame.* Where's the Princess?
"*Gage.* Oh, my honour'd lords,
May I presume with reverence to ask
What mean these arms? Why do you thus begirt
A poor weak lady, near at point of death?" &c.

In his "England's Elizabeth," Heywood thus speaks of this scene :—

"This which at the first was in the Queene but meere suspition, by Bishop Gardiner's aggravation grew after into her high indignation, in so much that a strict Commission was sent down to Ashridge, where shee then sojourned, to have her with all speede remove from thence, and brought up to London, there to answer all such criminal articles as could be objected against her. The charge was committed to Sir John Williams, Lord of Tame, Sir Edward Hastings, and Sir Thomas Cornwallis, all three Councillors of State, and for the better accomplishment of the service, a guard of 250 horsemen were attendant on them. The Princess was at the same time dangerously sicke, and even almost to death: the day was quite spent, and the evening come on, newes being brought unto her by her servants (much affrighted) that so great a strength had begirt her house, and in such a time when her innocence could not so much as dreame of any thing dangerous that might be suggested against her, it

---

[1] The London edition of 1631 has no engraver's name to the plate, which must have been added in 1632.

bred in her, howsoever, no small amazement; but ere shee could well recollect herselfe, a great rapping was heard at the gate. Shee sending to demand the cause thereof, in stead of returning an answer, the Lords stept into the house, without demanding so much as leave of the porter, and coming into the hall, where they met mistress Ashley, a gentlewoman that attended her, they willed her to inform her Lady that they had a message to deliver from the Queene. The Gentlewoman went up and told her what they had said, who sent them word back by her againe, that it being then an unseasonable time of the night, she in her bed and dangerously sicke, to intreate them, if not in courtesie, yet for modesties sake, to defer the delivery of their message till morning; but they, without further reply, as shee was returning to the Princesses chamber, followed her up stairs and pressed in after her, presenting themselves at her bedside. At which sight she was suddenly moved, and told them that she was not well pleased with their uncivill intrusion. They, by her low and faint speech perceiving her debilitie and weakness of body, desired her grace's pardon, (the Lord Tame speaking in excuse of all the rest) and told her they were sorry to find such infirmity upon her, especially since it was the Queenes express pleasure that the seventh of that present moneth shee must appeare before her Majestie, at her Court neere Westminster. To whom she answered that the Queene had not a subject in the whole kingdom more ready or willing to tender their service and loyalty to her Highnesse than herselfe; yet hoped, withall, in regard of her present disability, they who were eye-witnesses of her weake estate might in their own charity and goodness dispense with their extremity of hast; but the hast was such and the extremitie so great, that their Commission was to bring her either alive or dead. A sore Commission it is, said shee. Hereupon they consulted with her Physitians, charging them on their allegiance to resolve them whether she might be removed thence without imminent perill of her life. Upon conference together they returned answer that she might undergo that journey without death, though not without great danger, her infirmity being hazardfull, but not mortall. Their opinions thus delivered, they told her grace that she must of necessity prepare herselfe for the morrow's journey."—Page 96, &c.

It will be seen, by the above quotation, that Heywood uses some of the very same expressions he had employed in his play, and such will be found to be the case hereafter.

PAGE 15.

" *Enter* WINCHESTER, SUSSEX, HOWARD, TAME, CHANDOS,
and Constable.

" *Suss.* All forbear this place, unless the Princess.
" *Winch.* Madam,
We from the Queen are join'd in full commission.

[*They sit : she kneels.*

" *Suss.* By your favour, good my lord,
Ere you proceed.—Madam, although this place
Doth tie you to this reverence, it becomes not,
You being a Princess, to deject your knee," &c.

"Upon the Friday before Palme Sunday, the Bish. of Winchester, with nine more of the Council, convented her: being come before them, and offering to kneele, the Earl of Sussex would by no means suffer her, but commanded a chayre to bee brought in for her to sit on. Gardiner, Bishop of Winchester, and then Lord Chancellor, taking upon him to be the mouth of the rest, began very sharply to reprove her (as if she had beene already convicted) for having a hand in Wiat's rebellion; to whom she mildly answered, with a modest protestation, that shee had never had the least knowledge of his practice and proceedings: for proofe whereof, said shee, 'when Wyat at his death was by some malicious enemies of mine demanded whether I was any way knowing or accessary to his insurrection, even at the parting of life and body, having prepared his soule for heaven, when no dissimulation can be so much as suspected, even then he pronounced me guiltlesse. Besides the like question being demanded of Nicholas Throckmorton and James Crofts, at their Arraignment, I was likewise cleared by them; and being acquitted by all others, (my lords) would you have me to accuse my selfe?' After this she was questioned about a stirring in the West, rais'd by Sir Peter Carew, but answered to every particular so distinctly, that they could not take hold of the least circumstance, whereby they might any way strengthen their accusation: which Gardiner perceiving, told her that it would be her safest course to submit her selfe to the Queene, and to crave pardon of her gracious Majestie. Whereunto she answered that submission confest a crime, and pardon belonged to a delinquent, either of which being proved by her, she would then, and not till then, make use of his Grace's councell."—Page 108.

PAGE 18.

" Re-enter the Six Councillors.

" *Winch.* It is the pleasure of her Majesty
That you be straight committed to the Tower," &c.

" In the midst of these conceptions, Gardiner and the rest entred the chamber, and told her that it was her Majesties pleasure shee must instantly be conveyed to the Tower; that her household was dissolved, and all her servants discharged, except her Gentleman Usher, three Gentlewomen, and two Groomes, and that for her guard 200 northern white coates were appointed that night to watch about her lodging, and early the next morning to see her safely delivered into the custody of the Lieftenant of the Tower. The very name of Tower struck deepe horror into her, insomuch that the cheerful blood forsaking her fresh cheeks left nothing but ashy palenesse in her visage: shee spake these words— ' Alasse, my Lords, how comes it that I have so incensed my sister and Soveraigne? If it be held to be either criminal or capitall to be daughter to King Henry, sister to King Edward, of sacred memory, or to bee the next in blood to the Queene, I may then perhaps incurre as well the severity of censure as the rigour of sentence: but otherwise I here protest, before Heaven and you, I never, either in act or thought, have as yet trespassed against her Majesty; whose pleasure, if it be so that I must be confined, and my liberty restrained, my humble suite is unto you to be Petitioners on my behalfe unto her Majesty, that I may be sent unto some other place less notorious, that being a prison for Traytors and Malefactors in the highest degree.' The Earle of Sussex presently replied that her request was both just and reasonable, desiring the rest of the Lords to joine with him in her behalfe; whereupon the Bishop of Winchester cut him off, and told him that it was the Queenes absolute command, and her pleasure was unalterable."—Page 112.

PAGE 22.

" *Enter* GAGE, ELIZABETH, CLARENTIA, *her Gentlewoman.*

" *Gage.* Madam, you have stepp'd too short, into the
water," &c.

" She went ashore, and stepped short, into the water."—Page 122.
" She was then delivered to the charge of the Constable of the Tower,

who received her as his prisoner, and told her that he would show her to her lodgings; but she, being faint, began to complaine. The good Earle of Sussex, seeing her colour begin to faile, and she ready to sinke under his armes, called for a chayre; but the Constable would not suffer it to be brought. Then she sat down upon a faire stone, at which time there fell a great shower of raine: the heavens themselves did seeme to weepe at such inhumane usage. Sussex offered to cast his cloake about her, but she by no means would admit it. Then the Lieftenent, M. Bridges, intreated her to withdraw herselfe from the violence of the storm into some shelter, to whom she answered, ' I had better to sit here then in a worser place; for God knoweth, not I, whither you intend to lead me.' "— Page 123.

PAGE 24.

" *Re-enter* GAGE.

" *Gage.* My lords, the Princess humbly entreats
That her own servants may bear up her diet," &c.

" She was still kept close prisoner: the Constable of the Tower, then Lord Chamberlaine, would not suffer her own servants to carry up her dyet, but put it into the hands of rude and unmannerly soldiers, of which she complaining to her Gentleman Usher to have that abuse better ordered, the Lieftenant not only denyed to see it remedied, but threatened him with imprisonment, if he againe did but urge such a motion: neither would he suffer her own cooks to dress her dyet, but mingled his own servants with hers."—Page 144.

PAGE 30.

" *Enter* WINCHESTER, BENINGFIELD, *and* TAME.

" Madam, the Queen, out of her royal bounty,
Hath freed you from the thraldom of the Tower," &c.

" From thence (the Tower) [they] conveyed her to Woodstock, under the conduct and charge of Sʳ Henry Benningfield, with whom was joyned in Commission Sʳ John Williams, the Lord of Tame, and a hundred Northern Blew-Coates to attend them. These presenting themselves before her, she instantly apprehended them to be her new guardians; but at the sight of Sʳ Henry, whom she had never till that time seene, she sodainly started backe, and called to one of the lords, privately demanding of him, whether the scaffold were yet standing whereon the innocent

Lady Jane had not long before suffered? He resolved her that upon his honour it was quite taken downe, and that no memorial thereof was now remaining. Then shee beckoned another noble-man unto her, and asked of him what Sr Henry was? if he knew him? or if a private murther were committed to his charge, whether he had not the conscience to performe it? Answer was made that he was a man whom the Queene respected, and the Chancellour much favoured."—149.

PAGE 31.

"*Enter* ELIZABETH, BENINGFIELD, GAGE, *and* TAME.

"*Omnes*. The Lord preserve thy sweet grace!
"*Eliz.* What are these?
"*Gage.* The townsmen of the country," &c.

"The next morning, the country people, understanding which way she was to take her journey, had assembled themselves in divers places, some praying for her preservation and liberty : others presented her with nose-gayes, and such expression of their loves as the countrey afforded. The inhabitants of neighbour villages commanded the Bels to be rung; so that, with the loud acclamations of People, and the sound of Bels, the very ayre did eccho with the preservation of Elizabeth. Which being perceived by Sr Henry Benningfield, he called them rebels and traytors, beating them back with his truncheon. As for the ringers, he made their pates ring noone before they were released out of the stocks. The Princesse intreated him in their behalfe, and desired that he would desist from the rigour used to the people ...... At every word he spoke he still had up his Commission, which the Princess, taking notice of, told him he was no better than her Goaler. The very name of Goaler moved his patience; but knowing not how to mend himselfe, he humbly intreated her grace not to use that name, it being a name of dishonour, a scandall to his gentry.—' It is no matter,' (said she) ' Sir Henry; methinkes that name and your nature agree well together. Let me not heare of that word Commission : as oft as you but nominate your Commission, so oft will I call you Gaoler.' As she passed along towards Windsor, divers of her servants, seeing her passe so sadly by the way, being such as had been formerly discharged at the dissolution of her household, requested her Grace that she would vouchsafe to resolve them whither she was carryed? to whom she sent back an answer in these two narrow words, *Tanquam Ovis*.— Page 155.

PAGE 33.

" *Enter* BENINGFIELD *and* BARWICK, *his man.*

" *Bening.* Barwick, is this the chair of state ?" &c.

" Sir Henry being thus opposed, went up into a chamber, [at the house of Lord Tame] where was prepared a chayre, two cushions, and a rich carpet for her grace to sit in; but he, impatient to see such princely furniture for her entertainment, rather than hee should not bee taken notice of, like Sostratus, (*sic*) that set the Temple of Diana on fire onely to get him a name, hee presumptuously sate in the chayre, and called one Barwicke, his man, to pull off his bootes: which being known all over the house, he was well derided for his uncivill behaviour."—Page 160.

PAGE 35.

" *Enter* ELIZABETH, BENINGFIELD, CLARENTIA, TAME, GAGE, *and* BARWICK.

" *Eliz.* What fearful terror doth assail my heart ?" &c.

" He [her Gentleman Usher] found Sr Henry Benningfield and the Lord of Tame walking together, and having singled out the L. of Tame, told him that the cause of his coming was to be resolved, whether there were any secret plot intended against her grace that night or no? and if there were, that he and his fellows might know it, for they should account themselves happy to lose their lives in her rescue. The Lord of Tame nobly replyed that all such feares were needlesse, for if any such thing were attempted, he and all his followers would spend their blouds in her defence."—Page 153.

PAGE 37.

" [BENINGFIELD *takes a book and looks into it.*
" *Bening.* What has she written here ?"

" Before her departure from Woodstocke, having private notice that one M. Edmond Tremaine and M. Smithweeke were on the racke, and strictly urged to have accused her innocence, at her remove from thence shee wrote these two verses with her diamond in a glasse window:

' Much suspected by me,
Nothing proved can be,

' Quoth Elizabeth, Prisoner.'

Immediately after, order came down to bring her up to Court."—Page 188.

PAGE 40.

" *Winch.* Fellow, what then?—This warrant that concerns
The Princess' death shuffle amongst the rest:
He'll ne'er peruse' t."

"In the interim, a warrant came downe, under seale, for her execution.
Gardiner was the onely Dædalus and inventor of the engine; but Master
Bridges had the honour of her delivery; for he no sooner received the
warrant, but, mistrusting false play, presently made hast to the Queen.
Shee was no sooner informed, but renounced the least knowledge thereof,
called Gardiner and others whom she suspected before her, blamed them
for their inhumane usage of her, and tooke advice for her better security;
and thus was Achitophel's bloudy device prevented."—Page 146.

PAGE 44.

" *Queen.* Call the Princess!
" [*Exeunt for the Princess.* PHILIP *behind the arras.*"

" At last, after many letters written, long suite, and great friends made,
she was admitted to the presence of the Queene, whose face in two years
and more she had not seene. King Philip having before mediated for her,
and placed himselfe, unknowne to the Queene, behind the hangings of
Arras, on purpose to heare the discourse, her grace, about ten of the clocke
at night, was sent for into the presence . . . . . King Philip, having privately overheard the conference, was now fully settled in a good opinion
of her loyalty."—Page 197.

PAGE 54.

" *Sennet about the stage in order. The Mayor of London
meets them.*

" *Mayor.* I from this city, London, do present
This purse and Bible to your Majesty," &c.

" But being come to the Little Conduit in Cheape, shee perceived an
offer of Love, and demanded what it might signify? One told her Grace
that there was placed Time. 'Time, Time!' (said shee) 'and Time, I
praise my God, hath brought me hither. But what is that other with
the Booke?' She was resolved that it was Truth, the daughter of Time,
presenting the Bible in English, whereunto she answered, ' I thanke the

Citie for this guift above all the rest: it is a Booke which I will often
and often read over.'   Then she commanded Sir John Perrot, one of the
Knights that held up the Canopie, to go and receive the Bible; but being
informed that it was to bee let downe unto her by a silken string, shee
commanded him to stay.   In the interim, a Purse of gold was presented
by the Recorder, in the behalfe of the City, which shee received with her
owne hand."—Page 234.

Heywood was not born at the time when Elizabeth
came to the throne, but George Whetstone, a poet
and prose writer of eminence, was perhaps an eye-
witness of the ceremonial of the Queen's passage
through Cheapside; and in his "English Myrrour,"
1586, a work of much learning and interest, with
many minute points of history, he thus speaks of the
event above recorded :

"Her majestie was in Cheape side presented with the holy Bible in
English, which she reverently kissed and thankefully received, as hir
spirituall comfort, her temporall crosse, and godly counsellor.   The Maior
of London presented her majesty a thousand marks in a purse, with
humble petition that she would continue their good lady: she gave
answer, that if need required, she would willingly spend her blood in their
defence, which magnanimous saying all her after actions declared."—
Book II., p. 132.

The notes we have appended to the first part, "If
You know not Me, You know Nobody, or the Troubles
of Queen Elizabeth," will supply other necessary information, and serve farther to show the great incompleteness of the play.   Not a few other dramas of the
time are in the same condition, beginning with Marlowe's "Massacre at Paris," and coming down to
Dekker and Webster's "History of Sir Thomas
Wyat."   In the interval of about twenty years between these two dramas others were published, which,

like them, must have been printed from short-hand notes; and we consider it a point, now established beyond contradiction, that one of them was the unique edition of "Hamlet," in 1603, the property of the Duke of Devonshire.

Only a few words remain to be said, in explanation of the pages which conclude our present volume. They are cancels for Heywood's play, "A Woman killed with Kindness," which formed part of our last issue, in execution of our undertaking to complete an edition of the dramatic works of that poet. Our readers are aware, that that drama was unavoidably taken from "the third edition," although we were able to state, of our own knowledge, that a copy of the *first* edition once existed. When we reprinted "A Woman killed with Kindness," the great supplemental manuscript catalogue of books in the British Museum, in 153 volumes, had not been placed upon the shelves of the Reading-Room; and on taking down letter H, not very long after it was made accessible, we were surprised to see that it contained the first edition of which we had been in search for twenty years. It had been in the Museum since the date of Mr. Bright's sale, and we might have searched for it perhaps twenty years longer, had not recent circumstances occasioned the speedy preparation of the catalogue of the works acquired by our national library during the last four or five years.

The discovery of this original edition of 1607 has shown that not a few errors of importance had crept into the later impression of 1617; and to cure these

unavoidable defects, for which we, at least, were not
to blame, the cancels have been rendered necessary.
We have availed ourselves of this opportunity of
correcting one or two mistakes for which we are
responsible, but which those who are at all acquainted with the difficulty of editing old plays will
be prepared to excuse.

J. P. C.

A peal of Chambers.

[The following is the conclusion of the *second part* of "If You know not Me, You know Nobody," as it stands in the editions of 1606, 1609, and 1623. The edition of 1609 has the woodcut of Queen Elizabeth upon the title-page, which is not the case with the edition of 1606; and it is not found on the title-page of the edition of 1633, from which the last part of the drama is printed in the body of our volume.]

Enter Queen, HUNSDON, LEICESTER, *Drum, Colours, and Soldiers.*

Queen. A stand, there, lords! Whence comes this
    sound of shot?
Leic. Please it, your majesty, 'tis thought the fleet
Lately discover'd by your subject Fleming,
Riding along the coasts of France and Dunkirk,
Is met and fought with by your Admiral.
Queen. Heaven prosper his proceedings! Hark, my
    lord;
Still it increaseth. Oh, had God and nature
Given us proportion man-like to our mind,
We'd not stand here, fenc'd in a wall of arms,
But have been present in these sea alarms.
Huns. Your royal resolution hath created
New spirits in your soldiers' breasts, and made
Of one man three.

Enter a Post.

Queen. Make way, there!—What's the news?
Post. Your royal fleet bids battle to the Spaniards,
Whose number, with the advantage of the wind,
Gives them great odds; but the undaunted worth

And well known valour of your Admiral,
Sir Francis Drake, and Martin Frobisher,
Give us assured hope of victory.

    Queen. Where did the royal navies first encounter?

    Post. From Dover cliffs we might discern them join,
But such a cloud of smoke environ'd them,
We could discover naught of their proceedings;
For the great Spanish fleet had wind and tide.
God and good hearts stand on your Grace's side.

    Queen. There's for thy news.—He that first lent me
      breath,
Stand in the right of wrong'd Elizabeth.

    Omnes. God and his angels for Elizabeth.

Enter another Post.

    Queen. Welcome, a' God's name! What's the news,
      my friend?—
Alas, good man, his looks speak for his tongue.—
How stands the sea fight?

    Post. Most contrarious.
The Spanish fleet, cast in a warlike rank,
Like a half moon, or to a full bent bow,
Wait for advantage: when, amongst the rest,
Sir Martin Frobisher, blinded with smoke,
And fir'd in heart with emulating honour,
Gave the proud Spaniard a broadside of shot:
But being within the compass of their danger,
The distant corners of the crippled fleet
Circled him round. This valiant Frobisher,
With all his brave and gallant followers,
Are folded in death's arms.

    Queen. If he survive,
He shall be nobly ransom'd: if he die,
He lives an honour to his nation.—
How fares our Admiral?

Post. Bravely he fights;
Directs with judgment, and with heedful care
Offends the foe.   England ne'er bred
Men that at sea fight better managed.

Queen. It cheers my blood; and if my God be pleased,
For some neglected duty in ourself,
To punish us with loss of them at sea,
His will be done: yet will we pray for them.
If they return, ourself will be the first
Will bid them welcome.—What says valiant Leicester?
Thou wilt not leave me, wilt thou?   Dost thou look
     pale?—
What says old Hunsdon?—Nay; I'll speak thy part.
Thy hand, old Lord; I am sure I have thy heart.

          [*A noise within, crying,* " A Frobisher !"

          Enter a Captain.

Queen. Then, let both heart and hand
Be bravely used, in honour of our land.—
Before thou speak'st, take that: if he be dead,
A Queen will see his funeral honoured.

Cap. When the foes' ships
Had grasp'd his ships within a steelly girdle,
The valiant Captain, overcharg'd with her,
Having no room for cowardice or fear,
Gave all his ordinance a gallant charge,
Cheer'd up his soldiers, mann'd up his fights,
And standing barehead bravely on the deck,
When dangerous shot, as thick as April hail,
Dropp'd by his ears, he wav'd his warlike sword,
And, with a bold defiance to the foe,
The watchword given, his ordinance let fly
With such a fury, that it broke their ranks,
Shatter'd their sides, and made their warlike ships
Like drunkards reel, and tumble side to side.

But to conclude, such was the will of Heaven,
And the true spirit of that gentleman,
That, being thought hopeless to be preserved,
Yet, in war's despite, and all the Spaniards' scoff,
He brought his ship and soldiers bravely off.

Queen. War's spite, indeed! and we, to do him right,
The ship he sail'd in, fought in, call Warspite.—
Now, noble soldiers, rouse your hearts, like me,
To noble resolution: if any here
There be that love us not, or harbour fear,
We give him liberty to leave our camp
Without displeasure.
Our army's royal, so be equal our hearts;
For with the meanest here I'll spend my blood,
And so to lose it count my only good.—
A march! lead on! we'll meet the worst can fall:
A maiden Queen will be your General.

*They march one way out. At the other door, Enter
    Sir* FRANCIS DRAKE, *with colours and ensigns taken
    from the Spaniards.*

What mean these Spanish ensigns, in the hands
Of English subjects?

Drake. Honourable Queen,
They show that Spaniards' lives are in the hands
Of England's sovereign.

Queen England's God be prais'd!
But prithee, Drake—for well I know thy name,
And I'll not be unmindful of thy worth—
Briefly rehearse the danger of the battle.
Till Furbisher was rescued we have heard.

Drake. The danger after that was worse than then.
Valour a' both sides strove to rise with honour:
As is a pair of balance, once made even,
So stood the day, inclin'd to neither side.

Sometimes we yielded; but like a ram
That makes returnment to redouble strength,
Then forc'd them yield; when our Lord Admiral
Following the chase, Pedro, their Admiral,
With many knights and captains of account,
Were by his noble deeds ta'en prisoners,
And under his conduct are safely kept,
And are by this time landed at St. Margaret's:
From whence they mean to march along by land,
And at St. James' he'll greet your Majesty.
These Spanish ensigns, tokens of our conquest,
Our captains took from off their batter'd ships.
Such as stood out, we sunk; such as submitted,
Tasted our English mercy, and survive,
Vassals and prisoners to your sovereignty.

   Queen. Next under God your valours have the praise !
Dismiss our camp, and tread a royal march
Towards St. James', where, in martial order,
We'll meet and parley our Lord Admiral,
And set a ransom of his prisoners.
As for those ensigns, see them safely kept;
And give commandment to the Dean of Paul's
He not forget, in his next learned sermon,
To celebrate this conquest at Paul's Cross;
And to the audience in our name declare
Our thanks to Heaven in universal prayer:
For, tho' our enemies be overthrown,
'Tis by the hand of Heaven, and not our own.
On ! sound a call !—Now, loving countrymen,
Subjects, and fellow soldiers, that have left
Your weeping wives, your goods, and children,
And laid your lives upon the edge of death,
For good of England and Elizabeth,
We thank you all.　Those that for us would bleed,
Shall find us kind to them, and to their seed.

We here dismiss you, and dismiss our camp.
Again we thank you: pleaseth God we live,
A greater recompence than thanks we'll give.
   All. Our lives and livings for Elizabeth!
   Queen. Thanks; general thanks.—
Towards London march we to a peaceful throne:
We wish no wars, yet we must guard our own.
                            [Exeunt.

FINIS.

IF YOU KNOW NOT ME,

YOU KNOW NO BODIE;

OR

The troubles of Queene ELIZABETH.

DRAMATIS PERSONÆ.[1]

PHILIP of Spain.
GARDINER, Bishop of Winchester.
Constable of the Tower.
Lord Chamberlain.
SUSSEX.
TAME.
CHANDOS.
HOWARD.
Sir HENRY BENINGFIELD.
Sir HENRY CAREW.
Sir JOHN BROCKET.
Sir WILLIAM SENTLOW,
GRESHAM.
Lord Mayor, &c., of London.
GAGE.
DODDS.
BARWICK.
Doctors OWINE and WENDITH.
Sergeant Trumpeter.
Pursuivant.
Clown.
Englishman and Spaniard.
Cardinal POLE (in the Dumb Show).

MARY, Queen of England.
Princess ELIZABETH.
CLARENTIA.
Gentlemen, Gentlewomen, Soldiers, Servants, Attendants, Three
Poor Men, Cook, Pantler, Boy, &c.

[1] Not prefixed to the old editions.

IF YOU KNOW NOT ME, YOU KNOW NOBODY;

OR,

THE TROUBLES OF QUEEN ELIZABETH.

Enter SUSSEX *and Lord Chamberlain.*

Suss. Good morrow, my good Lord Chamberlain.

L. Cham. Many good morrows to my good Lord of
Sussex.

Suss. Who's with the Queen, my lord?

L. Cham. The Cardinal of Winchester, the Lord
of Tame, the good Lord Chandos; and, besides, Lord
Howard, Sir Henry Beningfield, and divers others.

Suss. A word, my lord, in private.

Enter TAME *and* CHANDOS.

Chand. Touching the Queen, my lord, who now sits
    high,

What thinks the realm of Philip, th' Emperor's son,

A marriage by the Council treated of?

Tame. Pray God 't prove well.

Suss. Good morrow, lords.

Tame. Good morrow, my good Lord of Sussex.

Chand. I cry your honour's mercy.

L. Cham. Good morrow to the Lords of Tame and
    Chandos.

Tame. The like to you, my lord. As you were
    speaking———

Enter Lord HOWARD *and Sir* HENRY BENINGFIELD.

Bening. Concerning Wyat and the Kentish rebels,
Their overthrow is past: the rebel dukes,
That sought by all means to proclaim Queen Jane,
Chiefly Northumberland, for Guilford's sake
He forc'd his brother duke into that war;
But each one had his merit——

How. Oh, my lord,
The law proceeded 'gainst their great offence,
And 'tis not well, since they have suffered judgment,
That we should raise their scandal, being dead:
'Tis impious, not by true judgment bred.

Suss. Good morrow, my lord; good morrow, good
    Sir Henry.

Bening. Pardon, my lord, I saw you not till now.

L. Cham. Good morrow, good Lord Howard.

How. Your honours. The like to you, my lords.

Tame. With all my heart, Lord Howard.

L. Cham. Forward, I pray.

Suss. The Suffolk men, my lord, were to the Queen
The very stairs by which she did ascend:
She's greatly bound unto them for their loves.

Enter Cardinal of Winchester.

Winch. Good morrow, Lords. Attend the Queen into
the presence.

Suss. Your duties, lords.   [*Exeunt omnes.*

Enter TAME *bearing the purse,* CHANDOS *the mace,*
    HOWARD *the sceptre,* SUSSEX *the crown: then, the*
    Queen; after her GARDINER, SENTLOW, GAGE, *and*
    attendants.

Queen. By God's assistance, and the power of Heaven,
We are instated in our brother's throne;

And all those powers that warr'd against our right,
By help of Heaven and your friendly aid,
Dispers'd and fled, here we may sit secure.
Our heart is joyful, lords; our peace is pure.

Enter DODDS.

Dodds. I do beseech your majesty, peruse
This poor petition.
    Queen. Oh, Master Dodds,
We are indebted to you for your love.
You stood us in great stead, even in our ebb
Of fortune, when our hopes were near declined,
And when our state did bear the lowest sail,
Which we have reason to requite, we know.—
Read his petition, my good Lord Cardinal.
    Dodds. Oh, gracious sovereign! let my lord, the
        duke,
Have the perusing of it,
Or any other that is near your grace.
He will be to our suit an opposite.
    Winch. And reason, fellow.—Madam,
Here is a large recital and upbraiding
Of your highness' sovereignty: the Suffolk men,
That lifted you to the throne, and here possess'd you,
Claim your promise you made to them about religion.
    Dodds. True, gracious sovereign;
But that we do upbraid your majesty,
Or make recital of our deeds forepast,
Other than conscience, honesty, and zeal,
By love, by faith, and by our duty bound
To you, the true and next successive heir,
If you contrary this, I needs must say,
Your skilless tongue doth make our well-tun'd words
Jar in the Prince's ears; and of our text
You make a wrong construction. Gracious Queen,

Your humble subjects prostrate in my mouth
A general suit: when we first flock'd to you,
And made first head with you at Framlingham,
'Twas thus concluded, that we, your liegemen,
Should still enjoy our consciences, and use
That faith which in King Edward's days was held
Canonical.

    Winch. May't please your highness, note
The commons' insolence: they tie you to conditions,
And set limits to your liking.

    Queen. They shall know
To whom their faithful duties they do owe:
Since they, the limbs, the head would seek to sway,
Before they govern, they shall learn t'obey.
See it severely order'd, Winchester.

    Winch. Away with him! it shall be thoroughly
      scann'd;
And you upon the pillory three days stand.

                           [*Exit* DODDS.

    Bening. Has not your sister, gracious Queen, a hand
In these petitions? Well your highness knows,
She is a favourite of these heretics.

    Winch. And well remember'd. Is't not probable
That she in Wyat's expedition,
And other insurrection lately quell'd,
Was a confederate? If your highness
Will your own estate preserve, you must
Foresee fore danger, and cut off all such
As would your safety prejudice.

    Bening. Such is your sister, a mere opposite
To us in our opinion; and, besides,
She's next successive, should your majesty
Die issueless, which Heaven defend.

    Omnes. Which Heaven defend.

    Bening. The state of our religion would decline.

Queen. My lords of Tame and Chandos,
You two shall have a firm commission seal'd
To fetch our sister, young Elizabeth,
From Ashridge, where she lies, and with a band
Of armed soldiers to conduct her up
To London, where we will hear her.

Sent. Gracious Queen,
She only craves but to behold your face,
That she might clear herself
Of all supposed treason, still protesting
She is as true a subject to your grace,
As lives this day.

Winch. Do you not hear with what a saucy impudence
This Sentlow here presumes?

Queen. Away with him! I'll teach him know his
      place;   [*Exit* SENTLOW.
To frown when we frown, smile on whom we grace.

Winch. 'Twill be a means to keep the rest in awe,
Making their sovereign's brow to them a law.

Queen. All those that seek our sister's cause to favour,
Let them be lodged.

Winch. Young Courtenay, Earl of Devonshire, seems
      chiefly
To affect her faction.

Queen. Commit him to the Tower,
Till time affords us and our Council breathing space.—
                    [*A horn within.*
Whence is that Post?

Enter Lord Constable, with letters.

Const. My sovereign, it is from Southampton.

Queen. Our secretary, unseal them,
And return us present answer of the contents.
What's the main business?
           [*She speaks to the Lord Constable.*

Const. That Philip, Prince of Spain,
Son to the Emperor, is safely arrived,
And landed at Southampton.

Queen. Prepare to meet him, lords, with all our pomp.

How. Prepare you, lords, with our fair Queen to ride;
And his high princely state let no man hide.

Queen. Set forward, lords: this sudden news is sweet;
Two royal lovers on the mid way meet.   [*Exeunt omnes.*

Enter Master GAGE *and a Gentlewoman.*

Gage. Good morrow, mistress.   Came you from the
Princess?

Gentlew. Master Gage, I did.

Gage. How fares her grace?

Gentlew. Oh, wondrous crazy, gentle Master Gage.
Her sleeps are all unquiet, and her head
Beats, and grows giddy with continual grief.

Gage. God grant her comfort, and release her pain.
So good a lady few on earth remain.

Enter the Clown.

Clown. Oh, arm! arm! arm!

Gage. How now! what's the matter?

Clown. Oh Lord! the house is beset: soldiers are as
hot as fire, are ready to enter every hole about the
house; for as I was a'top of the stack, the sound of the
drum hot me such a box on the ear, that I came tum-
bling down the stack, with a thousand billets a'top on
me.   Look about, and help, for God's sake!

Gage. Heaven guard the Princess! grant that all be
well!
This drum, I fear, will prove her passing bell.

Enter TAME *and* CHANDOS, *with Soldiers, drum, &c.*

Tame. Where's the Princess?

Gage. Oh, my honour'd lords,
May I presume with reverence to ask
What mean these arms ?   Why do you thus begirt
A poor weak lady, near at point of death.

Chand. Resolve the Princess we must speak with her.

Gentlew. My lords,
Know, there is no admittance to her presence
Without the leave first granted from herself.

Tame. Go, tell her we must, and will.

Gentlew. I'll certify so much.   [*Exit.*

Gage. My lords, as you are honourably born,
As you did love her father, or her brother,
As you do owe allegiance to the Queen,
In pity of her weakness and low state,
With best of favour her commiserate.

Re-enter Gentlewoman.

Gentlew. Her grace entreats you but to stay till morn,
And then your message shall be heard at full.

Chand. 'Tis from the Queen, and we will speak with
her.

Gentlew. I'll certify so much.

Tame. It shall not need.—Press after her, my lord.

Enter ELIZABETH, *in her bed. Doctor* OWINE *and
Doctor* WENDITH.

Eliz. We are not pleas'd with your intrusion, lords.
Is your haste such, or your affairs so urgent,
That suddenly, and at this time of night,
You press on me, and will not stay till morn ?

Tame. Sorry we are, sweet lady, to behold you
In this sad plight.

Eliz. And I, my lords, not glad.
My heart, oh, how it beats !

Chand. Madam,

Our message, and our duty from our Queen,
We come to tender you.   It is her pleasure
That you, the seventh day of this month, appear
At Westminster.

    Eliz. At Westminster?   My lords, no soul more
        glad than I
To do my duty to her majesty;
But I am sorry at the heart.—My heart!
Good doctor, raise me.   Oh, my heart!—I hope, my
        lords,
Considering my extremity and weakness,
You will dispense a little with your haste.

    Tame. Doctor Owine and Doctor Wendith,
You are the Queen's physicians, truly sworn
On your allegiance:
As before her highness you will answer it,
Speak, may the Princess be remov'd with life?

    Dr. Ow. Not without danger, lords, yet without
        death.
Her fever is not mortal; yet you see
Into what danger it hath brought the Princess.

    Chand. Is your opinion so?

    Dr. Wend. My judgment is,
Not deadly, but yet dangerous.
No sooner shall she come to take the air
But she will faint; and, if not well prepared
And attended, her life is in much danger.

    Tame. Madam, we take no pleasure to deliver
So strict a message.

    Eliz. Nor I, my lords, to hear
A message delivered with such strictness.
Well, must I go?

    Chand. So says the Queen.

    Eliz. Why, then, it must be so.

    Tame. To-morrow, early, then, you must prepare.

Eliz. 'Tis many a morrow since my feeble legs
Felt this my body's weight.—Oh, I shall faint!
And if I taste the rawness of the air,
I am but dead; indeed, I am but dead.
'Tis late: conduct these lords unto their chambers,
And cheer them well, for they have journied hard,
Whilst we prepare us for to-morrow's journey.

 Chand. Madam, the Queen hath sent her litter for
  you.

 Eliz. The Queen is kind, and we will strive with
  death
To tender her our life.
We are her subject, and obey her hest.
Good night: we wish you what we want—good rest.

         [Exeunt omnes.

 Enter Queen MARY, PHILIP, *and all the Nobles but*
    TAME *and* CHANDOS.

 Queen. Thus, in the face of Heaven, and broad eye
Of all the multitude,
We give a welcome to the Spanish Prince.—
Those plausive shouts, which give you entertain,
Echo as much to the Almighty's ears,
And there they sound with pleasure, that excels
The clamorous trumpets and loud ringing bells.

 Phil. Thrice excellent and ever gracious Princess,
Doubly famous for virtue and for beauty,
We embrace
Your large-stretch'd honours with the arms of love.
Our royal marriage, treated first in heaven,
To be solemniz'd here, both by God's voice
And by our love's consent, we thus embrace.
Now Spain and England, two populous kingdoms
That have a long time been oppos'd

In hostile emulation, shall be at one.
This shall be Spanish England, ours English Spain.

        [Flourish.

 Queen. Hark the redoubling echoes of the people !
How it proclaims their loves, and welcome to this
   union.

 Phil. Then, here, before the pillars of the land,
We do embrace and make a public contract.
Our souls are joyful: then, bright heaven, smile,
Whilst we proclaim our new-united style.

 Queen. Read, Sussex.

 Suss. (*reads*). "Philip and Mary, by the grace of
God, King and Queen of England, Spain, France, and
Ireland; King and Queen of Naples, Sicilia, Leon, and
Arragon; Arch-duke and Duchess of Austria, Bur-
gundy, of Brabant, Zealand, of Holland: Prince and
Princess of Sweave; Count and Countess of Has-
burghe, Marlorca, Sardinia, of the firm land and the
main ocean-sea; Palatines of Jerusalem, of Hainault;
Lord and Lady of Freezland, and of the Isles; and
Governor and Governess of all Africa and Asia."

 Omnes. Long live the King and Queen !　*[Flourish.*
 King and Qu. We thank you all.

 L. Const. When please your highness to solemnize
   this your nuptials ?

 Queen. The twenty-fifth day of this month, July.

 Phil. It likes us well.　But, royal Queen, we want
One lady at this high solemnity:
We have a sister call'd Elizabeth,
Whose virtues, and endowments of the mind,
Have filled the ears of Spain.

 Winch. Great are the causes, now too long to say,
Why she, my sovereign, should be kept away.

 Const. The Lords of Tame and Chandos are returned.

Enter TAME *and* CHANDOS, *and* GAGE.

Queen. How fares our sister! Is she come along?

Tame. We found the Princess sick, and in great
    danger;
Yet did we urge our strict commission:
She much entreated that she might be spared
Until her health and strength might be restored.

Chand. Two of your highness' doctors we then called,
And charged them, as they would answer it,
To tell the truth, if that our journey's toil
Might be no prejudice unto her life,
Or if we might with safety bring her thence.
They answered, that we might. We did so.
Here she is, to do her duty to your majesty.

Queen. Let her attend: we will find a time to hear
    her.

Phil. But, royal Queen, yet, for her virtues' sake,
Deem her offences, if she have offended,
With all the lenity a sister can.

Queen. My Lord of Winchester, my Lord of Sussex,
Lords Howard, Tame, and Chandos,
Take you commission to examine her
Of all supposed crimes.—So, to our nuptials.

Phil. What festival more royal hath been seen,
Than 'twixt Spain's Prince, and England's royal Queen?
                          [*Exeunt.*

Enter ELIZABETH, *her Gentlewoman, and three household*
Servants.

Eliz. Is not my gentleman-usher yet returned?

Gentlew. Madam, not yet.

Eliz. O, God! my fear hath been
Good physic; but the Queen's displeasure, that
Hath cur'd my body's imperfection,

Hath made my heart sick, brain sick, and sick even to
    death.
What are you?

   1 *Serv.* Your household officers and humble servants,
Who, now your house, fair Princess, is dissolved,
And quite broke up, come to attend your grace.

   Eliz. We thank you, and are more indebted to your
    loves
Than we have power or virtue to requite.
Alas! I am all the Queen's, yet nothing of myself;
But God and innocence,
Be you my patrons, and defend my cause.—
Why weep you, gentlemen?

   Cook. Not for ourselves: men are not made to weep
At their own fortunes. Our eyes are made of fire;
And to extract water from fire is hard.
Nothing but such a Princess' grief as yours,
So good a lady, and so beautiful, so absolute a mistress,
And perfect, as you ever have been,
Have power to do't: your sorrow makes us sad.

   Eliz. My innocence yet makes my heart as light
As my front's heavy. All that Heaven sends is welcome.
Gentlemen, divide these few crowns amongst you:
I am now a prisoner, and shall want nothing.
I have some friends about her majesty
That are providing for me all things, all things;
Ay, even my grave; and being possess'd of that,
I shall need nothing. Weep not, I pray;
Rather, you should rejoice. If I miscarry
In this enterprise, and you ask why,
A virgin and a martyr both I die.

Enter GAGE.

   Gage. He that first gave you life, protect that life
From those that wish your death.

Eliz. What's my offence? who be my accusers?

Gage. Madam, that the Queen and Winchester best
    know.

Eliz. What says the Queen unto my late peti-
    tion?

Gage. You are denied that grace:

Her majesty will not admit you conference.

Sir William Sentlow, urging that motion,

Was first committed, since sent to the Tower.

Madam, in brief, your foes are the Queen's friends,

Your friends her foes.

Six of the Council are this day appointed

To examine you of certain articles.

Eliz. They shall be welcome. My God, in whom I
    trust,

Will help, deliver, save, defend the just.

Enter WINCHESTER, SUSSEX, HOWARD, TAME,
    CHANDOS, *and Constable.*

Suss. All forbear this place, unless the Princess.

Winch. Madam,

We from the Queen are join'd in full commission.

                       [*They sit: she kneels.*

Suss. By your favour, good my lord,

Ere you proceed.—Madam, although this place

Doth tie you to this reverence, it becomes not,

You being a Princess, to deject your knee.—

A chair there!

Eliz. My duty with my fortunes doth agree,

And to the Queen, in you, I bend my knee.

Suss. You shall not kneel where Sussex sits in
    place.—

The chamber-keeper! A chair, there, for her grace!

Winch. Madam, perhaps you censure hardly

That was enforc'd in this commission.

Eliz. Know you your own guilt, my good Lord
    Chancellor,
That you accuse yourself?   I think not so:
I am of this mind—no man is my foe.
    Winch. Madam,
I would you would submit unto her highness.
    Eliz. Submit, my Lord of Winchester!   'Tis fit
That none but base offenders should submit.
No, no, my lord: I easily spy your drift:
Having nothing whereon you can accuse me,
Do seek to have myself myself betray;
So by myself my own blood should be spilt.
Confess submission, I confess a guilt.
    Tame. What answer you to Wyat's late rebellion?
Madam, 'tis thought that you did set them on.
    Eliz. Who is't will say so?   Men may much sus-
    pect,
But yet, my lord, none can my life detect.
I a confederate with those Kentish rebels!
If I e'er saw, or sent to them, let the Queen take my
    head.
Hath not proud Wyat suffer'd for his offence?
And in the purging both of soul and body for Heaven,
Did Wyat then accuse Elizabeth?
    Suss. Madam, he did not.
    Eliz. My reverend lord, I know it.
    How. Madam, he would not.
    Eliz. Oh, my good lord, he could not.
    Suss. The same day
Throgmorton was arraign'd in the Guildhall,
It was impos'd on him, whether this Princess
Had a hand with him, or no: he did deny it—
Clear'd her fore his death, yet accus'd others.
    Eliz. My God be praised!
This is news but of a minute old.

Chand. What answer you to Sir Peter Carew, in the
  West—
The Western rebels?
 Eliz. Ask the unborn infant: see what that will
  answer;
For that and I are both alike in guilt.
Let not by rigour innocent blood be spilt.
 Winch. Come, madam; answer briefly to these trea-
  sons.
 Eliz. Treason, my lord! If it be treason
To be the daughter to the eighth Henry,
Sister to Edward, and the next of blood
Unto my gracious sovereign, now the Queen,
I am a traitor: if not, I spit at treason.
In Henry's reign, this law could not have stood.
Oh, God! that we should suffer for our blood!
 Const. Madam,
The Queen must hear you sing another song,
Before you part with us.
 Eliz. My God doth know,
I can no note but truth; that with heaven's King
One day in choirs of angels I shall sing.
 Winch. Then, madam, you'll not submit?
 Eliz. My life I will, but not as guilty.
My lords, let pale offenders pardon crave:
If we offend, law's rigour let us have.
 Winch. You are stubborn.—Come, let's certify the
  Queen.
 Tame. Room for the lords, there! [*Exeunt Council.*
 Eliz. Thou Power Eternal, Innocents' just guide,
That sways the sceptre of all monarchies,
Protect the guiltless from these ravening jaws,
That hideous death present by tyrants' laws:
And as my heart is known to thee most pure,
Grant me release, or patience to endure!

Enter GAGE *and Servants.*

Gage. Madam, we, your poor, humble servants,
Made bold to press into your grace's presence,
To know how your cause goes.

   Eliz. Well, well; I thank my God, well.
How can a cause go ill with innocents?
For they to whom wrongs in this world are done,
Shall be rewarded in the world to come.

Re-enter the six Councillors.

   Winch. It is the pleasure of her majesty,
That you be straight committed to the Tower.

   Eliz. The Tower! For what?

   Winch. Moreover, all your household servants
We have discharg'd, except this gentleman, your usher,
And this gentlewoman: thus did the Queen command.
And for your guard, an hundred northern white-
      coats
Are appointed to conduct you thither.
To-night, unto your chamber: to-morrow, early,
Prepare you for the Tower. Your barge stands ready
To conduct you thither.   *[She kneels.*

   Eliz. Oh, God, my heart! A prisoner in the Tower?
Speak to the Queen, my lords, that some other place
May lodge her sister; that's too vile, too base.

   Suss. Come, my lords, let's all join in one petition to
      the Queen,
That she may not be lodg'd within the Tower.

   Winch. My lord, you know it is in vain;
For the Queen's sentence is definitive,
And we must see't perform'd.

   Eliz. Then, to our chamber, comfortless and sad:
To-morrow to the Tower—that fatal place,
Where I shall ne'er behold the sun's bright face.

Suss. Now, God forbid! a better hap Heaven send.
Thus men may mourn for what they cannot mend.

[*Exeunt omnes.*

Enter three white-coat Soldiers, with a jack of beer.

1 *Sold.* Come, my masters, you know your charge.
'Tis now about eleven: here we must watch till morning, and then carry the Princess to the Tower.

2 *Sold.* How shall we spend the time till morning?

3 *Sold.* Mass, we'll drink, and talk of our friends.

2 *Sold.* Ay, but, my friend, do not talk of State
matters.

1 *Sold.* Not I: I'll not meddle with the State. I
hope this a man may say, without offence—prithee,
drink to me.

3 *Sold.* With all my heart, i'faith: this a man might
lawfully speak. But now, faith, what wast about to
say?

1 *Sold.* Mass, I say this—that the Lady Elizabeth is
both a lady and Elizabeth; and if I should say she were
a virtuous princess, were there any harm in that?

2 *Sold.* No, by my troth, there's no harm in that.
But beware of talking of the Princess. Let's meddle
with our kindred; there we may be bold.

1 *Sold.* Well, sirs, I have two sisters, and the one
loves the other, and would not send her to prison for a
million. Is there any harm in this? I'll keep myself
within compass, I warrant you; for I do not talk of the
Queen: I talk of my sisters. I'll keep myself within
my compass, I warrant you.

3 *Sold.* Ay, sir; but that word sister goes hardly
down.

1 *Sold.* Why, sir, I hope a man may be bold with his
own. I learned that of the Queen. I'll keep myself
within compass, I'll warrant you.

2 Sold. Ay, but, sir, why is the Princess committed?

1 Sold. It may be, she doth not know herself. It may be, the Queen knows not the cause. It may be, my Lord of Winchester does not know. It may be so: nothing's unpossible to God. It may be, there's knavery in monkery: there's nothing unpossible. Is there any harm in that?

2 Sold. Shoemaker, you go a little beyond your last.

1 Sold. Why? In saying nothing's unpossible to God? I'll stand to it. For saying a truth's a truth? I'll prove it. For saying there may be knavery in monkery? I'll justify it. I do not say there is, but may be. I know what I know: he knows what he knows. Marry, we know not what every man knows.

3 Sold. My masters, we have talk'd so long, that I think 'tis day.

1 Sold. I think so too.— Is there any harm in all this?

2 Sold. No harm i' th' world.

3 Sold. And I think by this time the Princess is ready to take her barge.

1 Sold. Come, then, let's go. Would all were well. Is there any harm in all this? but, alas!
Wishes and tears have both one property;
They show their love that want the remedy.

        [Exeunt omnes.

 Enter WINCHESTER *and* BENINGFIELD.

Winch. Did you not mark what a piteous eye she cast
To the Queen's window, as she pass'd along?
Fain she would have stay'd, but that I caused
The bargemen to make haste and row away.

Bening. The bargemen were too desperate, my lord,
In staying till the water was so low;
For then, you know, being underneath the bridge,

The barge's stern did strike upon the ground,
And was in danger to have drown'd us all.

 Winch. Well, she hath scap'd that danger. Would
  she but

Conform herself in her opinion,
She only might rely upon my love,
To win her to the favour of the Queen.

 Bening. But that will never be: this is my censure;
If she be guilty in the least degree,
May all her wrongs survive and light on her:
If other ways, that she be clear'd. Thus, both ways
I wish her down, or else her state to raise.

Enter SUSSEX, TAME, HOWARD, CHANDOS, *and* GAGE.

 Suss. Why doth the Princess keep her barge so
  long?

Why lands she not? Some one go see the cause.

 Gage. That shall be my charge, my lord.

           [*Exit* GAGE.

 Suss. Oh, me! my lords, her state is wondrous
  hard.

I've seen the day my hand I'd not have lent
To bring my sovereign's sister to the Tower.
Good my lords, stretch your commission
To do this Princess but some little favour.

 Chand. My lord, my lord,
Let not the love we bear the Princess
Incur the Queen's displeasure: 'tis no dallying with
Matters of State. Who dares gainsay the Queen?

 Suss. Marry a God, not I; no, no, not I:
Yet who shall hinder these my eyes to sorrow
For her sorrow? By God's marry dear,
That the Queen could not, though herself were here.
My lords, my lords, if it were held foul treason
To grieve for her hard usage, by my soul,

My eyes would hardly prove me a true subject.
But 'tis the Queen's pleasure, and we must obey ;
But I shall mourn, should the King and Queen say nay.

Re-enter GAGE.

Gage. My grieved mistress humbly thus entreats,
For to remove back to the common stairs,
And not to land where traitors put to shore.
Some difference she entreats your honours make
'Twixt crystal fountains and foul, muddy springs;
'Twixt those that are condemned by the law,
And those whom treason's stain did never blemish.
Thus she attends your answer; and sits still,
Whilst her wet eyes full many a tear did spill.
Suss. Marry a God, 'tis true, and 'tis no reason.—
Launch, bargeman !—
Good lady land where traitors use to land,
And 'fore her guilt be prov'd ?   God's marry, no,
An the Queen wills it that it should be so.
Chand. My lord, you must look into our commis-
sion.
No favours granted, she of force must land :
'Tis a decree which we cannot withstand.
So tell her, Master Gage.   [*Exit* GAGE.
Suss. As good a lady as e'er England bred.
Would he that caus'd this woe had lost his head!

Enter GAGE, ELIZABETH, *and* CLARENTIA, *her Gentlewoman.*

Gage. Madam, you have stepp'd too short, into the
water :
Eliz. No matter where I tread.
Would where I set my foot there lay my head!
Land traitor like?   My foot's wet in the flood;
So shall my heart, ere long, be drench'd in blood.

Enter Constable.

Winch. Here comes the Constable of the Tower.—
This is your charge.

    Const. And I receive my prisoner.—Come, will you
      go?

    Eliz. Whither, my lord? unto a grate of iron,
Where grief and care my poor heart shall environ?
I am not well.

    Suss. A chair for the Princess!

    Const. Here's no chair for prisoners.
Come, will you see your chamber?

    Eliz. Then, on this stone, this cold stone, will I sit.
I needs must say, you hardly me entreat,
When for a chair this hard stone is my seat.

    Suss. My lord, you deal too cruelly with the Princess.
You knew her father; she's no stranger to you.

    Tame. Madam, it rains.

    Suss. Good lady, take my cloak.

    Eliz. No; let it alone. See, gentlemen,
The piteous heavens weep tears into my bosom.
On this cold stone I sit, rain in my face;
But better here than in a worser place,
Where this bad man will lead me.
Clarentia, reach my book.
Now, lead me where you please, from sight of day,
Or in a dungeon I shall see to pray.

           [*Exeunt* ELIZABETH, GAGE, CLARENTIA,
                and Constable.

    Suss. Nay, nay, you need not lock and bolt so fast;
She is no starter.—Honourable lords,
Speak to the Queen she may have some release.

Re-enter Constable.

    Const. So, so. Let me alone, let me alone to coop her.

I'll use her so, the Queen shall much commend
My diligent care.

How. Where have you left the Princess?

Const. Where she is safe enough, I warrant you.
I have not granted her the privilege
Of any walk or garden, or to ope
Her window's casements to receive the air.

Suss. My lord, my lord, you deal without respect,
And worse than your commission can maintain.

Const. My lord, I hope I know mine office well,
And better than yourself within this place:
Then, teach not me my duty.   She shall be us'd so still;
The Queen commands, and I'll obey her will.

Suss. But if this time should alter, mark me well,
Could this be answer'd?   Could it, fellow peers?
I think not so.

Const. Tush, tush! the Queen is young, likely to bear
Of her own body a more royal heir.

Re-enter GAGE.

Gage. My lords, the Princess humbly entreats,
That her own servants may bear up her diet.
A company of base, untutor'd slaves,
Whose hands did never serve a princess' board,
Do take that privilege.

Const. 'Twas my appointment, and it shall be so.

Suss. God's marry, dear, but it shall not be.
Lord Howard, join with me: we'll to the King.

Enter Soldiers, with dishes.

Gage. Stay, good my lords: for instance, see, they come.
If this be seemly, let your honours judge.

Suss. Come, come, my lords: why do you stay so long?
The Queen's high favour shall amend this wrong.

      [*Exeunt omnes, præter Constable and* GAGE.

Enter Soldiers, with more dishes. GAGE *takes one from them.*

Gage. Untutor'd slave, I'll ease thee of this burden.
Her highness scorns
To touch the dish her servants bring not up.

Const. Presume to touch the dish, I'll lodge thee there,
Where thou shalt see no sun for one whole year.
　　　　　　　　　　[*Exeunt Constable and Soldiers.*

Gage. I would to God you would, in any place
Where I might live from thought of her disgrace!
Oh! thou all-seeing heavens, with piteous eye
Look on the oppressions of their cruelty.
Let not thy truth by falsehood be oppress'd,
But let her virtues shine, and give her rest.
Confound the slights and practice of those men,
Whose pride does kick against the seat of Heaven.
Oh! draw the curtains from their filthy sin,
And make them loathe the hell which they live in.
Prosper the Princess, and her life defend:
A glorious comfort to her troubles send.
If ever thou hadst pity, hear my prayer,
And give releasement to a Princess' care.　　　　[*Exit.*

A DUMB SHOW.

Enter six, with torches. TAME *and* CHANDOS, *bare-headed;* PHILIP *and* MARY *after them; then* WIN-CHESTER, BENINGFIELD, *and Attendants. At the other door,* SUSSEX *and* HOWARD. SUSSEX *delivers a petition to the King, the King receives it, shows it to the Queen; she shows it to* WINCHESTER *and to* BEN-INGFIELD; *they storm: the King whispers to* SUSSEX, *and raises him and* HOWARD; *gives them the petition: they take their leaves, and depart. The King whispers a little to the Queen. Exeunt.*

Enter Constable and GAGE.

Gage. The Princess thus entreats you, honour'd lord;
She may but walk in the Lieutenant's garden,
Or else repose herself in the Queen's lodgings.
My honour'd lord, grant this, as you did love
The famous Henry, her deceased father.

Const. Come, talk not to me, for I am resolved
Nor lodging, garden, nor Lieutenant's walks,
Shall here be granted: she's a prisoner.

Gage. My lord, they shall.

Const. How shall they, knave?

Gage. If the Queen please, they shall.
A noble and right reverend councillor
Promis'd to beg it of her Majesty;
And, if she say the word, my lord, she shall.

Const. Ay; if she say the word, it shall be so.
My Lord of Winchester speaks the contrary;
So do the clergy: they are honest men.

Gage. My honoured lord, why should you take de-
            light
To torture a poor lady, innocent?
The Queen, I know, when she shall hear of this,
Will greatly discommend your cruelty.
You serv'd her father, and he lov'd you well:
You serv'd her brother, and he held you dear;
And can you hate the sister he best loved?
You serve her sister; she esteems you high,
And you may live to serve her, ere you die.
And, therefore, good my lord, let this prevail:
Only the casements of her window ope,
Whereby she may receive fresh, gladsome air.

Const. Oh! you preach well to deaf men: no, not I.
So letters may fly in; I'll none of that.
She is my prisoner; and if I durst,

But that my warrant is not yet so strict,
I'd lay her in a dungeon, where her eyes
Should not have light to read her prayer-book.
So would I danger both soul and body,
'Cause she an alien is to us Catholics:
Her bed should be all snakes, her rest despair:
Torture should make her curse her faithless prayer.

Enter SUSSEX, HOWARD, *and Servants.*

Suss. My lord, it is the pleasure of the Queen
The prisoner Princess should have all the use
Of the Lieutenant's garden, the Queen's lodgings,
And all the liberty this place affords.

Const. What means her grace by this?

Suss. You may go ask her, an you will, my lord.
Moreover, 'tis her highness' farther pleasure,
That her sworn servants shall attend on her:
Two gentlemen of her ewery, two of her pantry,
Two of her kitchen, and two of her wardrobe,
Besides this gentleman, here, Master Gage.

Const. The next will be her freedom. Oh! this
mads me.

How. Which way lies the Princess?

Const. This way, my lord.

How. This will be glad tidings. Come, let's tell her
grace.

[*Exeunt omnes, præter Constable and* GAGE.

Gage. Wilt please your honour let my lady walk
In the Lieutenant's garden,
Or may but see the lodgings of the Queen,
Or ope the casements to receive fresh air?
Shall she, my lord? Shall she this freedom use?
She shall; for you can neither will nor choose.
Or shall she have some servants of her own,
To attend on her? I pray, let it be so;

And let your look no more poor prisoners daunt.
I pray, deny not what you needs must grant.

[Exit GAGE.

  Const. This base groom flouts me. Oh! this frets
   my heart:
These knaves will jet upon their privilege.
But yet I'll vex her: I have found the means.
I'll have my cooks to dress my meat with hers,
And every officer my men shall match.
Oh! that I could but drain her heart's dear blood.
Oh! it would feed me—do my soul much good.

Enter the Clown, beating a Soldier.

[*Exeunt.*

Enter Cook, beating another Soldier.

  Const. How now! what means the fellow?
  Cook. Audacious slave, presuming in my place!
  Const. Sir, 'twas my pleasure, and I did command
   it.
  Cook. The proudest he that keeps within the Tower
Shall have no eye within my private office.
  Const. No, sir? Why, say 'tis I.
  Cook. Be it yourself, or any other here,
I make him sup the hottest broth I have.
  Const. You will not.
  Cook. Zounds! I will:
I have been true to her, and will be still. [*Exit.*
  Const. Well; I have this amended, ere't be long,
And venge myself on her for all their wrong. [*Exit.*

Enter a Boy, with a nosegay.

  Boy. I have got another nosegay for my young lady.
My lord said I should be soundly whipped,
If I were seen to bring her any more;
But yet I'll venture once again, she's so good.

Oh! here's her chamber: I'll call and see if she be
  stirring.
Where are you, lady?

  Eliz. (*at the casement*]. Welcome, sweet boy: what
    hast thou brought me there?

  Boy. Madam, I have brought you another nosegay,
But you must not let it be seen; for, if it be,
I shall be soundly whipp'd: indeed, la, indeed, I shall.

  Eliz. God a mercy, boy! Here's to requite thy love.
                                             [*Exit* ELIZ.

Enter Constable, SUSSEX, HOWARD, *and Attendants.*

  Const. Stay him, stay him!—Oh! have I caught you,
    sir?
Where have you been?

  Boy. To carry my young lady some more flowers.

  How. Alas, my lord! a child. Pray, let him go.

  Const. A crafty knave, my lords.—Search him for
    letters.

  Suss. Letters, my lord! It is impossible.

  Const. Come, tell me what letters thou carried'st her,
I'll give thee figs and sugar-plums.

  Boy. Will you, indeed? Well, I'll take your word,
For you look like an honest man.

  Const. Now, tell me what letters thou deliveredst.

  Boy. Faith, gaffer, I know no letters but great A,
B, and C: I am not come to K yet.
Now, gaffer, will you give me my sugar-plums?

  Const. Yes, marry will I.—Take him away:
Let him be soundly whipp'd, I charge you, sirrah.

Enter ELIZABETH, GAGE, *and* CLARENTIA.

  Eliz. They keep even infants from us: they do well.
My sight they have too long barr'd, and now my smell.
This Tower hath made me fall to housewif'ry:

I spend my labours to relieve the poor.
Go, Gage; distribute these to those that need.

Enter WINCHESTER, BENINGFIELD, *and* TAME.

Winch. Madam, the Queen, out of her royal bounty,
Hath freed you from the thraldom of the Tower,
And now this gentleman must be your guardian.

Eliz. I thank her : she hath rid me of a tyrant.
Is he appointed now to be my keeper?—
What is he, lords?

Tame. A gentleman in favour with the Queen.

Eliz. It seems so, by his charge.—But tell me,
 Gage,
Is yet the scaffold standing on Tower Hill,
Whereon young Guildford and the Lady Jane
Did suffer death?

Gage. Upon my life, it stands not.

Eliz. Lord Howard, what is he?

How. A gentleman, though of a stern aspect ;
Yet mild enough, I hope your grace will find.

Eliz. Hath he not, think you, a stretch conscience ;
And if my secret murder should be put
Into his hands,
Hath he not heart, think you, to execute?

How. Defend it, Heaven; and God Almighty's hand
Betwixt your grace and such intendments stand.

Bening. Come, madam ; will you go?

Eliz. With all my heart.—Farewell, farewell :
I am freed from limbo, to be sent to hell.

　　　　　　　　　　　　　　　　[Exeunt omnes.

Enter Cook and Pantler.

Cook. What storm comes next? this hath dispers'd us
 quite,
And shatter'd us to nothing.

Though we be denied the presence of our mistress,
Yet we will walk aloof, and none control us.

 Pant. Here will she cross the river: stand in her
  eye,
That she may take some notice of our neglected duties.

   Enter three poor men.

 1. Come: this way, they say, the sweet Princess
comes. Let us present her with such tokens of good
will as we have.

 2. They say she's such a virtuous Princess, that she'll
accept a cup of cold water; and I have even a nosegay
for her grace. Here she comes.

Enter ELIZABETH, BENINGFIELD, GAGE, *and* TAME.

 Omnes. The Lord preserve thy sweet grace!
 Eliz. What are these?
 Gage. The townsmen of the country, gather'd here
To greet your grace, hearing you pass'd this way.
 Eliz. Give them this gold, and thank them for their
  loves.
 Bening. What traitor knaves are gather'd here, to
  make
A tumult?
 Omnes. Now, the Lord bless thy sweet grace!
 Bening. If they persist, I charge you, soldiers, stop
their mouths.
 Eliz. It shall not need.
The poor are loving, but the rich despise;
And though you curb their tongue, spare them their
  eyes.—
Your love my smart allays not, but prolongs:
Pray for me in your hearts, not with your tongues.—
See, see, my lord: look, I have still'd them all.
Not one amongst them but debates my fall.

Tame. Alas, Sir Harry, these are honest countrymen,
That much rejoice to see the Princess well.

Bening. My lord, my lord, my charge is great.

Tame. And mine as great as yours.   [*Bells.*

Bening. Hark, hark, my lord? What bells are these?

Gage. The townsmen of this village,
Hearing her highness was to pass this way,
Salute her coming with this peal of bells.

Bening. Traitors and knaves! Ring bells,
When the Queen's enemy passeth through the town?
Go, set the knaves by the heels: make their pates
Ring noon, I charge thee, Barwick.   [*Exit* BARWICK.

Eliz. Alas, poor men! help them, thou God above!
Thus men are forc'd to suffer for my love.
What said my servants—those that stood aloof?

Gage. They deeply conjur'd me, out of their loves,
To know how your case goes, which these poor people
        second.

Eliz. Say to them, *tanquam ovis.*

Bening. Come, come away. This lingering will be-
        night us.

Tame. Madam, this night your lodging's at my house:
No prisoner are you, madam, for this night.

Bening. How! no prisoner?

Tame. No; no prisoner. What I intend to do,
I'll answer.—Madam, will't please you go?
                [*Exeunt* ELIZ., BENINGFIELD, *and* TAME.

Cook. Now, gentle master usher, what says my lady?

Gage. She thus did bid me say—*tanquam ovis.*
Farewell, I must away.   [*Exit* GAGE.

1. *Tanqus ovrus?* Pray, what's *tanqus ovrus*, neighbour?

2. If the priest were here, he'd smell it out straight.

Cook. Myself have been a scholar, and I understand
what *tanquam ovis* means.

We sent to know how her grace did fare:
She *tanquam ovis* said; even like a sheep
That's to the slaughter led.

1. *Tanqus ovrus:* that I should live to see *tanqus
ovrus.*

2. I shall ne'er love *tanqus ovrus* again, for this trick.

[*Exeunt omnes.*

Enter BENINGFIELD *and* BARWICK, *his man.*

Bening. Barwick, is this the chair of state?
Barw. Ay, sir; this is it.
Bening. Take it down, and pull off my boots.
Barw. Come on, sir.

Enter Clown.

Clown. Oh, monstrous! what a saucy companion's
this, to pull off his boots in the chair of state. I'll fit
you a pennyworth for it.
Bening. Well said, Barwick. Pull, knave.
Barw. Ah, ha, sir!
Bening. Well said: now it comes.

[*The Clown pulls the chair from under him.*
Clown. God's pity, I think you are down. Cry you
mercy.
Bening. What saucy, arrant knave art thou? How?
Clown. Not so saucy an arrant knave as your worship
takes me to be.
Bening. Villain! thou hast broken my crupper.
Clown. I am sorry 'tis no worse for your worship.
Bening. Knave! doest flout me?

[*He beats him out. Exeunt.*

Enter the Englishman and Spaniard.

Spa. The wall, the wall!
Eng. 'Sblood! Spaniard, you get no wall here, unless

you would have your head and the wall knocked together.

Spa. Signor Cavaliero d'Ingleterra, I must have the wall.

Eng. I do protest, hadst thou not enforced it, I had not regarded it; but, since you will needs have the wall, I'll take the pains to thrust you into the kennel.

Spa. Oh, base Cavaliero. My sword and poniard, well-tried Toledo, shall give thee the *imbrocado*.

Eng. Marry, and welcome, sir. Come on.

[*They fight: he hurts the Spaniard.*

Spa. Holo, holo! thou hast given me the *canvisado*.

Eng. Come, sir; will you any more?

Spa. Signor Cavaliero, look behind thee. A blade of Toledo is drawn against thee.

[*He looks back: he kills him.*

Enter PHILIP, HOWARD, SUSSEX, *Constable.*

Phil. Hand that ignoble groom!—Had we not
Beheld thy cowardice, we should have sworn
Such baseness had not follow'd us.

Spa. Oh, vostro mandato, grand Emperato.

How. Pardon him, my lord.

Phil. Are you respectless of our honour, lords,
That you would have us bosom cowardice?
I do protest, the great Turk's empire
Shall not redeem thee from a felon's death.
What place is this, my lords?

Suss. Charing Cross, my liege.

Phil. Then, by this cross, where thou hast done this
      murder,
Thou shalt be hang'd.—So, lords, away with him.

[*Exit Spaniard.*

Suss. Your grace may purchase glory from above,
And entire love from all your people's hearts,

To make atonement 'twixt the woful Princess
And our dread sovereign, your most virtuous Queen.

How. It were a deed worthy of memory.

Const. My lord, she's factious: rather could I wish
She were married to some private gentleman,
And with her dower convey'd out of the land,
Than here to stay, and be a mutiner.
So may your highness' state be more secure;
For whilst she lives, wars and commotions,
Foul insurrections, will be set abroach.
I think 'twere not amiss to take her head:
This land would be in quiet, were she dead.

Suss. Oh, my lord, you speak not charitably.

Phil. Nor will we, lords, embrace his heedless council.
I do protest, as I am King of Spain,
My utmost power I'll stretch to make them friends.
Come, lords, let's in: my love and wit I'll try,
To end this jar; the Queen shall not deny.

[*Exeunt omnes.*

Enter ELIZABETH, BENINGFIELD, CLARENTIA, TAME,
GAGE, *and* BARWICK.

Eliz. What fearful terror doth assail my heart?
Good Gage, come hither, and resolve me true:
In thy opinion, shall I outlive this night?
I prithee, speak.

Gage. Outlive this night! I pray, madam, why?

Eliz. Then, to be plain, this night I look to die.

Gage. Oh, madam, you were born to better fortunes.
That God that made you will protect you still
From all your enemies that wish you ill.

Eliz. My heart is fearful.

Gage. Oh, my honour'd lord,
As ever you were noble in your thoughts,
Speak, shall my lady outlive this night, or no?

Tame. You much amaze me, sir: else Heaven forefend.

Gage. For if we should imagine any plot
Pretending to the hurt of our dear mistress,
I and my fellows, though far unable are
To stand against your power, will die together.

Tame. And I with you would spend my dearest blood
To do that virtuous lady any good.
Sir Harry, now my charge I must resign:
The lady's wholly in your custody;
Yet use her kindly, as she well deserves.
And so I take my leave.—Madam, adieu. [*Exit* TAME.

Eliz. My honour'd lord, farewell: unwilling I
With grief and woe must continue.
Help me to some ink and paper, good Sir Harry.

Bening. What to do, madam?

Eliz. To write a letter to the Queen, my sister.

Bening. I find not that in my commission.

Eliz. Good jailor, urge not thy commission.

Bening. No jailor, but your guardian, madam.

Eliz. Then, reach me pen and ink.

Bening. Madam, I dare not: my commission serves not.

Eliz. Thus have you driven me off, from time to time,
Still urging me with your commission.
Good jailor, be not so severe.

Bening. Good madam, I entreat you, lose that name
Of jailor; 'twill be a by-word to me and my posterity.

Eliz. As often as you name your commission,
So often will I call you jailor.

Bening. Say, I should reach you pen, ink, and paper,
Who is't dare bear a letter sent from you?

Eliz. I do not keep a servant so dishonest
That would deny me that.

Bening. Whoever dares, none shall.

Gage. Madam, impose the letter to my trust.
Were I to bear it through a field of pikes,

And in my way ten thousand arm'd men ambush'd,
I'd make my passage through the midst of them,
And perforce bear it to the Queen your sister.

Bening. Body of me, what a bold knave's this!

Eliz. Gage, leave me to myself.—   [*Exit* GAGE.
Thou ever-living Power, that guid'st all hearts,
Give to my pen a true persuasive style,
That it may move my impatient sister's ears,
And urge her to compassionate my woe.   [*She writes.*

       [BENINGFIELD *takes a book, and looks into it.*

Bening. What has she written here?
" Much suspected by me, nothing proved can be.

                 [*He reads.*

Finis, quoth Elizabeth, the prisoner."
Pray God it prove so.   Soft! what book's this?
Marry a God! what's here? an English bible?
Sancta Maria, pardon this profanation of my heart!
Water, Barwick! water!   I'll meddle with't no more.

                [*Exit* BARWICK.

Eliz. My heart is heavy, and my heart doth close.
I am weary of writing—sleepy on the sudden.
Clarentia, leave me, and command some music
In the withdrawing chamber.   [*She sleeps.*

Bening. Your letter shall be forthcoming, lady.
I will peruse it, ere it 'scape me now.

            [*Exit* BENINGFIELD.

A DUMB SHOW.

Enter WINCHESTER, *Constable,* BARWICK, *and Friars:
at the other door, two Angels. The Friars step to her,
offering to kill her : the Angel drives them back. Exeunt.
The Angel opens the Bible, and puts it in her hand as
she sleeps. Exeunt Angels. She wakes.*

Eliz. Oh, God! how pleasant was this sleep to me!
Clarentia, saw'st thou nothing?

Clar. Madam, not I.
I ne'er slept soundlier for the time.
   Eliz. Nor heard'st thou nothing?
   Clar. Neither, madam.
   Eliz. Didst thou not put this book into my hand?
   Clar. Madam, not I.
   Eliz. Then, 'twas by inspiration.—Heaven, I trust,
With His eternal hand, will guide the just.
What chapter's this? " Whoso putteth his trust in
the Lord shall not be confounded."
My Saviour, thanks; on thee my hope I build:
Thou lov'st poor innocents, and art their shield.

Enter BENINGFIELD *and* GAGE.

   Bening. Here have you writ a long excuse, it
      seems,
But no submission to the Queen, your sister.
   Eliz. Should they submit that never wrought of-
      fence?
The law will always quit wrong'd innocence.—
Gage, take my letter: to the lords commend
My humble duty.
   Gage. Madam, I fly
To give this letter to her majesty.
Hoping, when I return,
To give you comfort that now sadly mourn.
[*Exeunt omnes, præter* BENINGFIELD.
   Bening. Ay, do write and send. I'll cross you
      still.
She shall not speak to any man alive,
But I'll o'erhear her: no letter, nor no token
Shall ever have access unto her hands,
But first I see it.
So, like a subject to my sovereign's state,
I will pursue her with my deadly hate.

Enter Clown.

Clown. Oh, Sir Harry! you look well to your office:
Yonder's one in the garden with the Princess.

Bening. How, knave, with the Princess? She parted
  even now.

Clown. Ay, sir, that's all one; but she no sooner came
into the garden, but he leap'd o'er the wall; and there
they are together, busy in talk, sir.

Bening. Here's for thy pains: thou art an honest
  fellow.

Go, take a guard, and apprehend them straight.

                                        [*Exit Clown.*

Bring them before me.—Oh! this was well found out.
Now will the Queen commend my diligent care,
And praise me for my service to her grace.
Ha! traitors swarm so near about my house?
'Tis time to look into't.—Oh, well said, Barwick.
Where's the prisoner?

Enter Clown, BARWICK, *and Soldiers, leading in a goat:*
  his sword drawn.

Clown. Here he is, in a string, my lord.

Bening. Lord bless us! Knave, what hast thou there?

Clown. This is he I told you was busy in talk with
the Princess. What a' did there, you must get out of
him by examination.

Bening. Why, knave, this is a beast.

Clown. So may your worship be, for any thing that I
know.

Bening. What art thou, knave?

Clown. If your worship does not remember me, I
hope your worship's crupper doth. But if you have
any thing to say to this honest fellow, who, for his grey
head and reverend beard is so like, he may be akin to
you——

Bening. Akin to me? Knave, I'll have thee whipp'd.

Clown. Then, your worship will cry quittance with my posteriors, for misusing of yours.

Bening. Nay, but dost thou flout me still?

[*He beats him.   Exeunt.*

Enter WINCHESTER, GRESHAM *with paper; Constable with a Pursuivant.*

Gresh. I pray your honour to regard my haste.

Winch. I know your business, and your haste shall
  stay.—

As you were speaking, my Lord Constable——

Const. When as the King shall come to seal these writs.

Gresh. My lord, you know his highness' treasure
  stays,

And cannot be transported this three months,

Unless that now your honour seal my warrant.

Winch. Fellow, what then?—This warrant, that concerns

The Princess' death, shuffle amongst the rest:

He'll ne'er peruse't.

Gresh. How! the Princess' death? Thanks, Heaven,
  by whom

I am made a willing instrument her life to save,

That may live crown'd when thou art in thy grave.

[*Exit* GRESHAM.

Winch. Stand ready, Pursuivant, that when 'tis
  sign'd,

Thou may'st be gone, and gallop with the wind.

Enter PHILIP, SUSSEX, *and* GAGE.

Phil. Our Chancellor, lords. This is our sealing
  day:

This our State's business.—Is our signet there?

Enter HOWARD *and* GRESHAM, *as he is sealing.*

How. Stay your imperial hand! Let not your seal
    imprint
Death's impress in your sister's heart.

Phil. Our sister's heart! Lord Howard, what means
    this?

How. The Chancellor, and that injurious lord
Can well expound the meaning.

Winch. Oh, chance accurst! how came he by this
    notice?
Her life is guarded by the hand of Heaven,
And we in vain pursue it.

Phil. Lord Chancellor, your dealing is not fair.
See, lords, what writ offers itself
To the impress of our seal.

Suss. See, my lord, a warrant
For the Princess' death, before she be convicted.
What juggling call you this? See, see, for God's sake.

Gage. And a pursuivant, ready to post
Away with it, to see it done with speed.
What flinty breast could brook to see her bleed?

Phil. Lord Chancellor, out of our prerogative
We will make bold to interline your warrant.

Suss. Who's plot was this?

How. The Chancellor's, and my Lord Constable's.

Suss. How was it revealed?

How. By this gentleman, Master Gresham, the King's
agent, here.

Suss. He hath show'd his love to the King and
    Queen's majesties,
His service to his country, and care of the Princess.

Gresh. My duty to them all.

Phil. Instead of charging of the Sheriffs with her,
We here discharge her keeper, Beningfield;

And where we should have brought her to the block,
We now will have her brought to Hampton Court,
There to attend the pleasure of the Queen.
The Pursuivant, that should have posted down
With tidings of her death, bear her the message
Of her reprieved life.—You, Master Gage,
Assist his speed.—A good day's work we ha' made,
To rescue innocence too soon betray'd. [*Exeunt omnes.*

Enter Clown and CLARENTIA.

Clown. Whither go you so fast, Mistress Clarentia?
Clar. A milking.
Clown. A milking! that's a poor office for a madam.
Clar. Better be a milkmaid free, than a madam in
    bondage.
Oh! hadst thou heard the Princess yesternight,
Sitting within an arbour, all alone,
To hear a milkmaid sing,
It would have mov'd a flinty heart to melt.
Weeping and wishing, wishing and weeping,
A thousand times she with herself debates
With the poor milkmaid to exchange estates.
She was a sempster in the Tower, being a Princess,
And shall I, her poor gentlewoman, disdain
To be a milkmaid in the country?
Clown. Troth, you say true: every one to his fortune,
As men go to hanging.   The time hath been
When I would have scorn'd to carry coals, but now,
But now the case is alter'd; every man
As far as his talent will stretch

Enter a Gentlewoman.

Gentlew. Where's Mistress Clarentia?   To horse, to
horse!   The Princess is sent for to the Court.   She's
gone already.   Come, let's after.

. *Clar.* The Princess gone, and I left here behind?
Come, come : our horses shall outstrip the wind.

Clown. And I'll not be long after you ; for I am sure
my curtal will carry me as fast as your double gelding.

[*Exeunt.*

Enter ELIZABETH *and* GAGE.

Eliz. I wonder, Gage, that we have stay'd so long
So near the Court, and yet have heard no news
From our displeased sister. This more affrights me
Than my former troubles. I fear this Hampton
    Court
Will be my grave.

Gage. Good madam, blot such thoughts out of your
    mind.
The lords, I know, are still about your suit,
And make no doubt that they will so prevail,
Both with the King and Queen, that you shall see
Their heinous anger will be turn'd to love.

Enter HOWARD.

How. Where is the Princess?
Eliz. Welcome, my good Lord Howard.
What says the Queen? Will she admit my sight?
How. Madam, she will : this night she hath appointed,
That she herself in person means to hear you.
Protract no time : then, come ; let's haste away.

[*Exeunt.*

Enter four torches. PHILIP, *the Queen,* WINCHESTER,
HOWARD, CHANDOS, BENINGFELD, *and attendants.*

Queen. Where is the Princess?
How. She waits your pleasure at the common
    stairs.
Queen. Usher her in by torch-light.

How. Gentlemen ushers and gentlemen pensioners,
  lights
For the Princess!   Attendance, gentlemen.
  Phil. For her supposed virtues, royal Queen,
Look on your sister with a smiling brow,
And if her fault merit not too much hate,
Let her be censur'd with all lenity.
Let your deep hatred end where it begun:
She hath been too long banish'd from the sun.
  Queen. Our favour shall be far 'bove her desert;
And she that hath been banish'd from the light,
Shall once again behold our cheerful sight.
You, my lord, shall step behind the arras,
And hear our conference.   We'll show her grace,
That there shines too much mercy in your face.
  Phil. We bear this mind: we errors would not feed,
Nor cherish wrongs, nor yet see innocents bleed.
  Queen. Call the Princess!
    [*Exeunt for the Princess*.   PHILIP *behind the arras*.

Enter all with ELIZABETH.

All forbear this place, except our sister, now.
                            [*Exeunt omnes*.
  Eliz. That God that rais'd you, stay you, and protect
You from your foes, and clear me from suspect.
  Queen. Wherefore do you cry?
To see yourself so low, or us so high?
  Eliz. Neither, dread Queen: mine is a womanish tear,
In part compell'd by joy, in part by fear.
Joy of your sight these brinish tears have bred,
And fear of my Queen's frown to strike me dead.
  Queen. Sister, I rather think they're tears of spleen.
  Eliz. You were my sister, now you are my Queen.
  Queen. Ay, that's your grief.
  Eliz. Madam, he was my foe,

And not your friend, that hath possess'd you so.
I am as true a subject to your grace,
As any lives this day.   Did you but see
My heart, it bends far lower than my knee.

> *Queen.* We know you can speak well. Will you
> submit?

Eliz. My life, madam, I will; but not as guilty.
Should I confess
Fault done by her that never did transgress?
I joy to have a sister Queen so royal:
I would it as much pleas'd your majesty,
That you enjoy a sister that's so true.
If I were guilty of the least offence,
Madam, 'twould taint the blood even in your face.
The treasons of the father, being noble,
Unnobles all his children: let your grace
Exact all torture and imprisonment,
Whate'er my greatest enemies can devise,
And they all have done their worst, yet I
Will your true subject, and true sister die.

> *Phil. (behind the arras).* Mirror of virtue and bright
> Nature's pride!

Pity it had been such beauty should have died.

> *Queen.* You'll not submit, but end as you begin?
> *Eliz.* Madam, to death I will, but not to sin.
> *Queen.* You are not guilty, then?
> *Eliz.* I think I am not.
> *Queen.* I am not of your mind.
> *Eliz.* I would your highness were.
> *Queen.* How mean you that?
> *Eliz.* To think as I think, that my soul is clear.
> *Queen.* You have been wrong imprisoned, then?
> *Eliz.* I'll not say so.
> *Queen.* Whate'er we think, arise and kiss our hand.

Say, God hath rais'd you friends.

Eliz. Then, God hath kept His promise.

Queen. Promise! why?

Eliz. To raise them friends that on His word rely.

Enter PHILIP.

Phil. And may the heavens applaud this unity:
Accurs'd be they that first procur'd this wrong.
Now, by my crown, you ha' been kept down too long.

Queen. Sister, this night yourself shall feast with me;
To-morrow for the country: you are free.—
Lights for the Princess! Conduct her to her chamber.
[Exit ELIZABETH.

Phil. My soul is joyful that this peace is made;
A peace that pleaseth heaven and earth and all,
Redeeming captive thoughts from captive thrall.
Fair Queen, the serious business of my father
Is now at hand to be accomplished:
Of your fair sight needs must I take my leave:
Return I shall, though parting cause us grieve.

Queen. Why should two hearts be forc'd to separate?
I know your business, but believe me, sweet,
My soul divines we never more shall meet.

Phil. Yet, fair Queen, hope the best: I shall return,
Who met with joy, though now sadly mourn.
[Exeunt PHILIP, Queen, and attendants.

Bening. What! droops your honour?

Winch. Oh! I am sick.

Const. Where lies your grief?

Winch. Where yours and all good subjects' else
      should lie,
Near at the heart. This confirmation I do greatly
      dread;
For now our true religion will decay.
I do divine, whoever lives seven year
Shall see no religion here but heresy.

Bening. Come, come, my lord, this is but for a show.
Our Queen, I warrant, wishes in her heart
Her sister Princess were without her head.

Winch. No, no, my lords: this peace is natural;
This combination is without deceit;
But I will once more write to incense the Queen.
The plot is laid: thus it shall be performed.
Sir Harry, you shall go attach her servant,
Upon suspicion of some treachery,
Wherein the Princess shall be accessary.
If this do fail, my policy is down.
But I grow faint: the fever steals on me:
Death, like a vulture, tires upon my heart.
I'll leave you two to prosecute this drift:
My bones to earth I give, to Heaven my soul I lift.

[*Exeunt Omnes.*

Enter GAGE and CLARENTIA.

Gage. Madam Clarentia, is my lady stirring?

Clar. Yes, Master Gage, but heavy at the heart,
For she was frighted with a dream this night.
She said she saw her sister was new married,
And sat upon a high imperial throne:
That she herself was cast into a dungeon,
Where enemies environ'd her about,
Offering their weapons to her naked breast;
Nay, they would scarcely give her leave to pray,
They made such haste to hurry her away.

Gage. Heaven shield my mistress, and make her
friends increase;
Convert her foes; estate her in true peace!

Clar. Then did I dream of weddings and of flowers.
Methought I was within the finest garden
That ever mortal eye did yet behold:
Then straight me thought some of the chief were pick'd

To dress the bride.   Oh! 'twas the rarest show
To see the bride come smiling 'longst the streets,
As if she went to happiness eternal.

Gage. Oh, most unhappy dreams! my fear is now
As great as yours : before it was but small.
Come, let's go comfort her that joys us all.   [*Exeunt.*

ENTER A DUMB SHOW: SIX TORCHES.

SUSSEX *bearing the crown,* HOWARD *bearing the sceptre,
the Constable the Mace,* TAME *the purse,* CHANDOS *the
sword :* PHILIP *and* MARY ; *after them the Cardinal*
POLE, BENINGFIELD, *and attendants.* PHILIP *and*
MARY *confer : he takes leave, and exit.· Nobles bring
him to the door and return ; she falls in a swoon ; they
comfort her.   A dead march.   Enter four with the
hearse of* WINCHESTER, *with the sceptre and purse
lying on it : the Queen takes the sceptre and purse, and
gives them to Cardinal* POLE.   *A sennet, and exeunt
omnes, præter* SUSSEX.

Suss. Winchester's dead.   Oh God! even at his death
He show'd his malice to the sweet young Princess.
God pardon him! his soul must answer all.
She is still preserved, and still her foes do fall.
The Queen is much besotted on these prelates,
For there's another rais'd, more base than he —
Pole, that arch [fiend], for truth and honesty.

Enter BENINGFIELD.

Bening. My lord of Sussex, I can tell ill news.
The Cardinal Pole, that now was firmly well,
Is suddenly fallen sick, and like to die.

Suss. Let him go.   Why, then, there's a fall of prelates.
This realm will never stand in perfect state,
Till all their faction be clear ruinate.

Enter Constable.

Const. Sir Harry, do you hear the whispering in
the court?
They say the Queen is crazy, very ill.
Suss. How heard you that?
Const. 'Tis common through the house.

Enter HOWARD.

How. 'Tis a sad court, my lord.
Suss. What's the matter? say, how fares the Queen?
How. Whether in sorrow for the King's departure,
Or else for grief at Winchester's decease,
Or else that Cardinal Pole is suddenly dead,
I cannot tell; but she's exceeding sick.
Suss. The State begins to alter.
How. Nay, more, my lord: I came now from the
Presence;
I heard the doctors whisper it in secret,
There is no way but one.
Suss. God's will be done. Who's with the Queen,
my lord?
How. The Duke of Norfolk, the Earl of Oxford,
The Earl of Arundell, and divers others:
They are withdrawn into the inward chamber,
There to take counsel, and entreat your presence.
Suss. We'll wait upon their honours. [*Exeunt omnes.*

Enter ELIZABETH, GAGE, *and* CLARENTIA, *above.*

Eliz. Oh, God! my last night's dream I greatly fear;
It doth presage my death.—Good Master Gage,
Look to the pathway that doth come from the Court:
I look each minute for Death's messenger.
Would he were here now, so my soul were pure,
That I with patience might the stroke endure.

E.

Gage. Madam, I see from far a horseman coming;
This way he bends his speed.   He comes so fast,
That he is cover'd with a cloud of dust;
And now I have lost his sight.   He appears again,
Making his way o'er hill, hedge, ditch, and plain.
One after him: they two strive,
As on the race they wager'd both their lives.
Another after him.

    Eliz. Oh, God! what means this haste?
Pray for my soul: my life cannot long last.

    Gage. Strange and miraculous! the first being at the
        gate,
His horse hath broke his neck, and cast his rider.

    Eliz. This same is but a prologue to my death.
My heart is guiltless, though they take my breath.

Enter Sir HENRY CAREW.

    Carew. God save the Queen!   God save Elizabeth!

    Eliz. God save the Queen; so all good subjects say:
I am her subject, and for her still pray.

    Carew. My horse did you allegiance at the gate,
For there he broke his neck, and there he lies,
For I myself had much ado to rise.
The fall hath bruis'd me, yet I live to cry,
God bless your grace! God bless your majesty!

    Gage. Long live the Queen! long live your majesty!

    Eliz. This news is sweet: my heart was sore afraid.
Rise thou, first baron that we ever made.

    Carew. Thanks to your majesty. Happy be my
        tongue,
That first breath'd right to one that had such wrong.

Enter Sir John BROCKET.

    Brock. Am I prevented in my haste? Oh, chance
        accurs'd!

My hopes did soothe me that I was the first.
Let not my duty be o'ersway'd by spleen;
Long live my sovereign, and God save the Queen!

    Eliz. Thanks, good Sir John: we will deserve your
        love.

Enter HOWARD.

    How. Though third in order, yet the first in love,
I tender my allegiance to your grace.
Live long, fair Queen; thrice happy be your reign!
He that instates you, your high state maintain!

    Eliz. Lord Howard, thanks; you ever were our
        friend:
I see your love continues to the end.
But chiefly thanks to you, my Lord of Hunsdon.

    How. Meaning this gentleman?

    Eliz. The very same:
His tongue was first proclaimer of our name.
And trusty Gage, in token of our grace,
We give to you a Captain Pensioner's place.

    How. Madam, the Council are here hard at hand.

    Eliz. We will descend, and meet them.

    Carew. Let's guard our sovereign, praising that
        power,
That can throw down and raise within an hour.

                  [*Exeunt omnes.*

Enter the Clown and one more, with faggots.

    Clown. Come, neighbour; come away: every man
his faggot and his double pot, for joy of the old Queen's
death.

        Let bells ring, and children sing,
        For we may have cause to remember
        The seventeenth day of November.

Enter Lord of TAME.

Tame. How now, my masters! what's here to do?

Clown. Faith, making bonfires, for joy of the new
Queen. Come, sir, your penny: an you be a true
subject, you'll battle with us your faggot. We'll be
merry, i'faith.

Tame. And you do well. And yet, methink, 'twere fit
To spend some funeral tears upon her hearse,
Who, while she liv'd, was dear unto you all.

Clown. Ay, but do you not know the old proverb?
We must live by the quick, and not by the dead.

Tame. Did you not love her father, while he liv'd,
As dearly as you e'er did love any,
And yet rejoiced at his funeral?
Likewise her brother you esteem'd him dear,
Yet, once departed, joyfully you sung.
Run to make bonfires, to proclaim your love
Unto the new, forgetting still the old:
Now she is gone, how you moan for her!
Were it not fit a while to moan her hearse,
And dutifully then rejoice the other?
Had you the wisest and the loving'st prince
That ever sway'd the sceptre in the world,
This is the love he shall have after life.
Let princes while they live have love, or fear, 'tis fit,
For after death there's none continues it.

Clown. By my faith, my masters, he speaks wisely.
Come, we'll to the end of the lane, and there we'll make
a bonfire and be merry.

1. Faith, agreed: I'll spend my halfpenny towards
another faggot, rather than the new Queen shall want
a bonfire.   [*Exeunt. Manet* TAME.

Tame. I blame you not, nor do I you commend,
For you will still the strongest side defend.   · [*Exit.*

A SENNET.

*Enter four Trumpeters: after them Sergeant Trumpeter,
with a mace; after him Purse-bearer.* SUSSEX, *with
the Crown;* HOWARD, [with] *the Sceptre; Constable,
with the Cap of Maintenance;* CHANDOS, *with the
Sword;* TAME, *with the Collar and a George. Four
Gentlemen, bearing the Canopy over the Queen; two
Gentlewomen, bearing up her train: six Gentlemen
Pensioners. The Queen takes state.*

Omnes. Long live, long reign our sovereign !

Eliz. We thank you all.

Suss. The imperial crown I here present your grace;
With it my staff of office, and my place.

Eliz. Whilst we this crown, so long your place enjoy.

How. The imperial sceptre here I offer up.

Eliz. Keep it, my lord; and with it be you High
Admiral.

Const. This Cap of Maintenance I present,
My state of office, and my utmost service.

Eliz. Your love we know.

Const. Pardon me, gracious madam: 'twas not spleen,
But that allegiance that I ow'd my Queen.
Madam, I serv'd her truly at that day,
And I as truly will your grace obey.

Eliz. We do as freely pardon, as you truly serve;
Only your staff of office we'll displace:
Instead of that, we'll owe you greater grace.

Enter BENINGFIELD.

Bening. Long live the Queen ! long live your majesty !
I have rid hard to be the first reporter
Of these glad tidings first, and all these here !

Suss. You are in your love as free as in your care:
You're come even just a day after the fair.

Eliz. What's he?   My jailor?

Bening. God preserve your grace!

Eliz. Be not asham'd, man: look me in the face.
Whom have you now to practise your strictness on?
For your kindness this I will bestow:
When we have one we would have hardly us'd,
And cruelly dealt with, you shall be the man.
This is a day of peace, not for vengeance fit:
All your good deeds we'll quit, all wrongs remit.—
Where we left off proceed.

Chand. The sword of Justice on my bended knee
I to your grace present.   Heaven bless your reign!

Eliz. This sword is ours; this staff is yours again.

Tame. This Garter, with the order of the George,
Two ornaments unto the crown of England,
I here present.

Eliz. Possess them still, my lord.— What offices bear
   you?

Gage. I?   Captain of your highness' Pensioners.

Brock. I, of your Guard.

Sergeant. I, Sergeant Trumpeter, present my mace.

Eliz. Some we intend to raise, none to displace.—
Lord Hunsdon, we will one day find a staff
To poise your hand: you are our cousin,
And deserve to be employed nearer our person.
But now to you, from whom we take this staff,
Since Cardinal Pole is now deceas'd and dead,
To show all malice from our breast is worn,
Before you let that Purse and Mace be borne.
And now to London, lords, lead on the way,
Praising that King that all kings else obey.

*Sennet about the stage in order.   The Mayor of London
meets them.*

Mayor. I from this city, London, do present

This purse and Bible to your Majesty.
A thousand of your faithful citizens,
In velvet coats and chains, well mounted, stay
To greet their royal sovereign on the way.

   Eliz. We thank you all; but first this book I kiss:
Thou art the way to honour, thou to bliss.
An English Bible! Thanks, my good Lord Mayor:
You of our body and our soul have care.
This is the jewel that we still love best;
This was our solace when we were distress'd.
This book, that hath so long conceal'd itself,
So long shut up, so long hid, now, lords, see,
We here unclasp: for ever it is free.
Who looks for joy, let him this book adore;
This is true food for rich men and for poor.
Who drinks of this is certain ne'er to perish:
This will the soul with heavenly virtue cherish.
Lay hand upon this anchor, every soul,
Your names shall be in an eternal scroll.
Who builds on this, dwells in a happy state;
This is the fountain, clear, immaculate.
That happy issue that shall us succeed,
And in our populous kingdom this book read,
For them, as for our own selves, we humbly pray,
They may live long, and blest.—So: lead the way!

FINIS.

NOTES AND VARIOUS READINGS

TO THE FIRST PART OF

IF YOU KNOW NOT ME, YOU KNOW NOBODY.

Page 4, line 6, *Into* that war.] *Unto* that war, edit. 1606.

Page 5, line 24, Made *to* them.] Edit. 1606 omits " to."

Page 5, line 33, Jar in the *Princes'* ears.] Jar in the *Princess* ears, edit. 1606, which may be right; but the change does not seem necessary, as the word " prince" was often, of old, applied to a queen. We follow the first edition, of 1605, in all cases where a change is not required by the obvious meaning of the poet.

Page 6, line 3, And made first head with you at Framlingham.] Queen Mary sought shelter in Framlingham Castle, while the Duke of Northumberland was endeavouring to enforce the claim of Lady Jane Grey. " When the Lady Mary received the news of her brother's death, having long before been acquainted with the Duke of Northumberland's secret practices, she judged it unsafe to remain near London, where her enemies were in full power; and, therefore, pretending a fear of the plague, by reason of the sudden death of one of her domestics, she withdrew from St. Edmund's Bury, (her abode at that time) and in one day came to Framlingham Castle, in the county of Suffolk, about four score miles from London, and not far from the sea; by which, if the extremity of her fears required it, she might have an easy passage to France . . . . . At the same time, news was brought that the people of Norfolk and Suffolk had taken their oaths to her."—Bishop Godwin, in Kennett, ii., 329. Stow says—" By this time word was brought to the Tower that the Lady Mary was fled to Framlingham Castle, in Suffolk, where the people of the country almost wholly resorted to her."—*Annales*, 1615, p. 1032. In the old copies of this play, the name of the place is printed Fromagham, according to the rustic and local pronunciation.

Page 6, line 25, And other *insurrection* lately quelled.] Later editions have *insurrections ;* but the reading of the first impression is probably the true one. This allusion to the quelling of Wyat and his adherents is a little premature: he was not subdued and taken until February, 1554; and these incidents formed the subject of a play by Dekker and Webster, which was printed very imperfectly in 1607; indeed, the Rev. Mr. Dyce (Webster's Works, ii., 251) is of opinion that not more than two-thirds of the piece, as it came from the pens of the authors, has been preserved in the printed copies. The library of the Duke of Devonshire contains an unique copy of an impression in 1612, hitherto unknown.

Page 7, line 16, Exit Sentlow.] Not marked in the old copies, but clearly necessary. We must suppose that Sir W. Sentlow, one of Elizabeth's faithful servants, is sent out under guard.

Page 7, line 22, Young Courtenay, Earl of Devonshire.] Edward Courtenay had been created Earl of Devon, (not Devonshire) according to Stow, (*Annales*, 1041) on 3rd September, 1553.

Page 7, line 29, Enter Constable, with letters.] The old copies omit to note his entrance with information regarding the Post, and with the letters brought by it.

Page 8, line 9, Enter Master Gage, and a Gentlewoman.] Of course, the scene here changes to Ashridge, where Elizabeth, as we have been already told, was residing.

Page 8, line 22, Soldiers *are* as hot as fire.] "Are" seems surplusage, but is not necessarily so, and the later copies here follow the reading of the earliest.

Page 9, line 23, Enter Elizabeth, in her bed.] Meaning, no doubt, that the Princess, ill in her bed, was thrust out upon the stage, and the scene immediately supposed to be a bed-room. So, in "A Woman Killed with Kindness," we have had, "Enter Mrs. Frankford in her bed:" see p. 160.

Page 11, line 8, Madam, the Queen hath sent her *litter* for you.] In the earliest edition, "litter" is misprinted *letter*, but it is corrected in subsequent impressions.

Page 11, line 16, Enter Queen Mary, Philip, &c.] The scene is here transferred to Winchester, whither Mary had gone to meet Philip, and where they were married.

Page 11, line 23, *That* excels.] So editions 1606, &c.; the first edition reads "*and* excels," which makes a false concord.

Page 12, line 12, Philip and Mary, by the grace of God, &c.] Stow gives their "style" as follows—"Philip and Mary, by the grace of God, King and Queen of England, France, Naples, Hierusalem, and Ireland, Defenders of the Faith, Princes of Spain and Sicily, Archdukes of Austrich, Dukes of Milan, Burgundy, and Brabant, Counties of Aspurge, Flanders, and Tyroll."—*Annales*, 1057. Bishop Godwin adds that the style was proclaimed in Latin, French, and English.

Page 12, line 26, The twenty-fifth day of this month, July.] St. James's day : Heywood is very particular and accurate in this date.

Page 13, line 24, What festival, &c.] These two lines, in edit. 1632, are made part of the Queen's speech.

Page 13, line 27, Enter Elizabeth, her *Gentlewoman*.] So the earlier impressions, but in that of 1632, *Gentleman* is misprinted for "Gentlewoman." The scene is here changed to London.

Page 14, line 19, And perfect, as you ever have been.] This line, like many others, is incurably defective, and edit. 1605 reads, "And perfect, as you ever have *delivered* been."

Page 14, line 30, In this enterprise, and *you ask* why.] And ask you why—edit. 1605.

Page 15, line 33, Madam, perhaps you censure hardly,

That was enforc'd in this commission.]

The meaning would seem to be, "Madam, perhaps, you censure, or think, hardly of us, that *were* enforced in this commission:" it only wants a slight alteration, to complete the verse and the sense : thus—

"Madam, perhaps, *of us* you censure hardly,

That *were* enforc'd in this commission."

Page 16, line 30, The same day

Throgmorton was arraign'd in the Guildhall.]

Stow says, "The 17th of April, were led to the Guildhall in London, to be arraign'd, Sir Nicholas Throckmorton and Sir James Croft, Robert Winter and Cuthbert Vaughan being also had thither to witness against them ; where that day no more was arraigned but Sir Nicholas Throckmorton, who, tarrying from seven o'clock in the morning until almost five at night, was by the verdict of the jury acquit: he pleaded not guilty, and that he was consenting to nothing, &c. But the jury which quit him was commanded to appear before the Council at an hour's warning, and the loss of £500 the piece."—*Annales*, 1055. We are to understand, from the text, that Wyat, not Throckmorton, cleared Elizabeth before his death.

Page 16, line 35, This is news but of a minute old.] It may be doubted whether this line belongs to Elizabeth, for in her confinement she would not know how old the news just communicated to her was: it was perhaps intended to be spoken by Sussex. Wyat was executed on 11th April, 1554.

Page 17, line 1, What answer you to Sir Peter Carew, in the West?]
"Within six days after [the trial of Robert Dudley], there was word
brought to the Court, how that Sir Peter Carow, Sir Gawine Carow, Sir
Thomas Deny, with divers other, were up in Devonshire, in the resisting
of the King of Spain's coming hither, and that they had taken the city of
Exeter, and castle there, into their custody."—Stow's *Annales*, p. 1044.

Page 18, line 6, How can a cause go ill with *innocents*?] Possibly,
innocence is the proper reading; but in the preceding page we have had
"innocents" used in the same way as here, and the old copies are uniform
in its favour.

Page 18, line 7, For they to whom.] So corrected in the later impressions: the first edition reads, "They that to whom," &c.

Page 18, line 11, That you be straight committed to the Tower.] Elizabeth was committed to the Tower, according to Stow, on the 18th of
March, being Palm Sunday. She was conducted thither by the Lord
Treasurer and the Earl of Sussex, who took her by water from Westminster.—*Annales*, p. 1054.

Page 19, line 15, With all my heart, *i'faith*.] Edit. 1605 has "With all
my hearty faith," and later impressions, "With all my heart, faith." It
is a trifle, but no doubt our text is the true reading.

Page 20, line 5, Nothing's unpossible *to God*.] Edit. 1605 has "to God,"
but those words were afterwards omitted—no doubt in consequence of
the statute against the use of oaths, and the name of the Creator, on the
stage, 3 Jac. I., c. 21. We have noted hereafter similar corrections elsewhere, but we have not thought it necessary to point them out.

Page 20, line 15, My masters, we have talked so long, that I think 'tis
day.] This may seem rather a large demand upon the imagination of the
audience, considering that there had been no intervening scene, and considering also that the talk of the "white-coated soldiers" had commenced on
the previous page, "about eleven" at night. The fact is, that at this period
of our stage, spectators were accustomed to allow such claims.

Page 22, line 13, Full many a tear *did* spill.] So edit. 1605: *doth*
spill, later editions; but both are wrong—one in tense, and the other in
number.

Page 22, line 18, *An* the Queen wills it that it should be so.] *i.e.*, *if*
the Queen wills it that it should be so. We only notice the passage for
the purpose of stating that, in old printing, *and* (as in this case) is often
used for "an."

Page 23, line 29, Nay, nay; you need not lock and bolt so fast.] We
give the stage-direction as in the old editions; and we may presume that

after Elizabeth has gone out with the Constable, the noise of locks and bolts is heard, though not expressed in the margin.

Page 25, line 7, *For* one whole year.] *In* one whole year, later editions.

Page 25, line 11, With piteous *eye*.] With piteous *eyes*, edit. 1606.

Page 25, line 16, Against *the* seat of Heaven.] Against *thy* seat of Heaven," edit. 1605.

Page 25, line 31, Gives them *the* petition.] Gives them *a* petition, edit. 1605.

Page 28, line 6, These knaves will *jet* upon their privilege.] The word "jet" hardly requires explanation. It is from *jetter*, French, and signifies to swagger, or throw oneself about, assuming false consequence. It is of constant occurrence in almost every old author.

Page 28, line 12, Enter the Clown, beating a Soldier. Exeunt.] *i.e.*, the Clown beats the Soldier across the stage, and they go out together.

Page 30, line 5, Hath freed you from the thraldom of the Tower.] Stow tells us, "On the 19th May, Lady Elizabeth was conveyed from the Tower of London, by water, to Richmond; from thence to Windsor; and so, by the Lord Williams, to Ricote, in Oxfordshire; and from thence to Woodstock."—*Annales*, 1056.

Page 30, line 7, I thank her, &c.] The necessary prefix of *Eliz.* is omitted before this speech, in edit. 1605.

Page 30, line 13, Is yet the scaffold standing on Tower Hill,

Whereon young Guildford and the Lady Jane
Did suffer death?]

Heywood here misrepresents the fact, for Lady Jane Grey was not executed on Tower Hill, but within the Tower, on 12th February, 1554-5.

Page 30, line 20, A *stretch* conscience.] A *stretch* conscience is the reading of edit. 1605, and there seems no sufficient reason for altering it to a "*stretch'd* conscience," as was done in subsequent impressions. Elizabeth, of course, means a conscience that will stretch.

Page 31, line 30, Your love my smart *allays* not.] Misprinted, in edit. 1605, "*alwaies* not."

Page 32, line 7, Hearing her highness *was to* pass this way.] Edit. 1605 omits the two words in italic. It also has *your* for "her," in this line and the next.

Page 33, line 8, Enter Beningfield, &c.] We must suppose that the scene here changes to the house of Lord Tame.

Page 33, line 17, Well *said*, Barwick.] "Well said," was, of old, often used for well *done*. See Shakespeare, edit. Collier, iii., 39; iv., 330; vi., 337, &c.

Page 33, line 30, Enter the Englishman and Spaniard.]   The scene is here transferred to London—to Charing Cross—where this rencontre is said to have occurred.

Page 34, line 16, He looks back: he kills him.]   *i.e.*, the Spaniard kills him: but we have not thought it expedient to alter the old stage-direction, which is intelligible enough.

Page 34, line 17.]   To these persons the old editions add, "and Gresham ;" but he says and does nothing.

Page 34, line 21, *Oh, vostro mandato, grand Emperato*.]   *Sic in orig.*; but perhaps we ought to read, *Al vuestro mandato, grande Emperador*. Heywood possibly thought that what he wrote would pass with his audience for sufficiently good Spanish; or, more probably, it was misprinted by the old typographer.

Page 34, line 33, Your grace may purchase *glory* from above.]   Edit. 1632 substitutes *honour* for "glory."

Page 35, line 7, Than here to stay, and be a *mutiner*.]   *Mutiner* is the old word, in the same way as *Enginer* in "Hamlet," act iii., sc. iv.—

> " For 'tis the sport, to have the *enginer*
>
> Hoist with his own petar."

Gabriel Harvey, in "Pierce's Supererogation," 1593, calls Nash "the dreadful enginer of phrases."   Modern editors (with one exception) have substituted "engineer," in the passage in "Hamlet," without reflecting what was the language of the time when Shakespeare wrote. *Engineer* did not come into use until afterwards; and we find Sir John Denham employing it in the reign of Charles II. (State Poems, i., 33)—

> " If thou art Minos, be a judge severe,
>
> And in's own maze confine the *Engineer*."

Page 36, line 23, Still urging me with your commission.]   This line is omitted in edit. 1632.

Page 37, line 5, *Exit Gage*.]   Necessary, but not in the old copies. In the next line, for "guid'st," edit. 1605 has *givest*.

Page 37, line 10, Beningfield takes a book, and looks into it.]   The probable meaning of this old stage-direction is, that after Beningfield has taken up the book, (which turns out to be a Bible in English) he over-looks and repeats what Elizabeth has written.   This couplet (which we have put in quotation) is imputed to Elizabeth, in Fox's "Acts and Monuments," and from thence Heywood may have derived it.

Page 37, line 18, Water, Barwick! water!]   *i.e.*, that Beningfield may wash himself from the profanation.   Nothing is said, in the old editions, of the *exit* of Barwick, and we are most likely to understand that it takes place here, just before the departure of his master: otherwise, we find him on the stage at the beginning of the scene, and the poet does not contrive to get him off.

Page 37, line 29, The *Friars step* to her.] In the old copies it stands, " The Friar steps to her;" but Friars have just been mentioned in the plural; and afterwards we have, " The Angel drives *them* back."

Page 38, line 19, The law will always *quit* wrong'd innocence.] *i.e.,* *acquit* wrong'd innocence : " quit" is more often used for requite.

Page 39, line 20, *His* sword drawn.] Probably Barwick had drawn his sword, but it is not easy to ascertain to whom the pronoun "his" applies here.

Page 40, line 2, *Then,* your worship, &c.] *When* your worship, &c., in some of the later editions.

Page 40, line 22, Thanks, Heaven.] Thanks *to* Heaven, edit. 1632.

Page 40, line 31, Our Chancellor, lords.] Gardiner had been appointed Lord Chancellor on 23rd August, 1553. See Lord Campbell's " Lives," ii., 54. Stow gives the same date. "The 23 of August, the Queen delivered the Great Seal to Doctor Gardener, Bishop of Winchester, and made him Lord Chancellor."—*Annales,* 1041.

Page 41, line 14, See, lords, what writ *offers* itself.] Edit. 1605, *affords* itself; edit. 1632, " What writs offer themselves."

Page 42, line 8, To rescue innocence *too soon* betray'd.] So edit. 1605 ; edit. 1632, *so near* betray'd.

Page 42, line 9, Enter Clown and Clarentia.] Of course, in the country, where Beningfield had the custody of Elizabeth.

Page 42, line 27, When I would have scorn'd to carry coals.] This phrase often occurs in our old writers, to indicate submission to injury, indignity, or unworthy office. After the notes upon " Romeo and Juliet," act i., sc. i, no further illustration can be required.

Page 43, line 3, I am sure my *curtal* will carry me as fast as your double gelding.] A " curtal" was a docked, or short-tailed horse: the Clown means to pun upon "double gelding" and double gilding.

Page 43, line 27, Enter four torches.] The scene changes to Hampton Court, in the neighbourhood of which Elizabeth had arrived in the preceding scene. Among the *dramatis personæ* present, the important character of "the Queen" is omitted in the old editions. This interview is supposed to occur at night.

Page 44, line 15, *That* there shines.] So edit. 1605: that of 1632 has, *For* there shines.

Page 44, line 30, And fear of my Queen's frown.] Our reading here is that of the later copies: edit. 1605 has, "*For* fear of my Queen's frown," which does not express what Elizabeth means, viz., that her tears were compelled in part by joy, and in part by fear.

Page 45, line 16, Unnobles all *his* children.]   All *your* children, edit. 1605.

Page 45, line 19, And they all have done their worst.]   The sense seems to require that we should read, "And *when* they have all done their worst," &c.   The addition also improves the measure, which, however, is generally so irregular as to be a very unsure guide.

Page 45, line 24, You'll not submit, but end as you begin?]   Edit. 1632 interpolates *then*, after "submit."

Page 45, line 34, Whate'er *we* think.]   Edit. 1632, Whate'er *you* think.

Page 46, line 4, Enter Philip.]   From behind the arras, where he had spoken two lines in admiration of Elizabeth.   Later editions, after the first, omit to notice the entrance of Philip, and none of them mention the return of Winchester, Beningfield, and the Constable, who take up the dialogue after Philip, the Queen, and their attendants, have withdrawn.

Page 46, line 18, Return I shall, &c.]   Philip went to Flanders on 4th September, 1555, and returned to England 23rd March, 1557.

Page 47, line 15, My bones to earth I give, &c.]   Bishop Gardiner died on 12th November after the departure of Philip to Flanders.

Page 47, line 28, Heaven *shield* my mistress.]   Heaven *bless* my mistress, edit. 1632.

Page 48, line 1, Oh! 'twas the *rarest* show.]   *Bravest* show, edit. 1632.

Page 48, line 3, As if *she* went.]   As if *we* went, edit. 1632.

Page 48, line 16, The Queen takes the sceptre and purse.]   It was "sceptre and purse" in the preceding line, but in this line edit. 1605 has "sceptre and *mace*."

Page 48, line 19, Oh, God! even at his death.]   So all subsequent impressions, but that of 1605 reads, "Oh, God! *upon* even at his death."

Page 48, line 25, Pole, that arch [fiend], for truth and honesty.]   Every old copy omits "fiend," or some such word, which we have added between brackets, as necessary both to meaning and measure.

Page 49, line 12, Or else that Cardinal Pole is suddenly dead.]   Cardinal Pole did not, in fact, die until some hours after Queen Mary: however, Heywood, like other play-poets of his day, did not profess to treat matters historically, but dramatically.   Stow (*Annales*, p. 1073) tells us that he died on the same day as Queen Mary.

Page 49, line 26, Enter Elizabeth, Gage, and Clarentia, *above*.] That is, as we may presume, in the balcony at the back of the old stage. Elizabeth was at Hatfield at the time of the death of her sister. The three bearers of the news of the accession of Elizabeth must have stood on the boards, and from thence addressed the Queen in the balcony above.

Page 50, line 27, Rise thou, first baron that we ever made.] Henry Carew, (or Carey) son and heir of William Carew, by Mary, daughter of the Earl of Wiltshire, and sister of Anne Boleyn, mother of Elizabeth, consequently first cousin to the new Queen, was not, in fact, created Baron Hunsdon until 13th January, 1559.

Page 51, line 26, Enter the Clown and one more, with faggots.] " One more " was the smallest number that would answer the purpose, and perhaps the largest number the company could spare.

Page 52, line 7, *And* yet, methink, 'twere fit.] *But* yet, methink, 'twere fit, edit. 1632.

Page 52, line 21, And dutifully *then* rejoice the other?] Edit. 1605 has, " And dutifully *there*," &c.

Page 52, line 33, Nor do *I you* commend.] Nor do you *much* commend, edit. 1632.

Page 53, line 1, A Sennet.] *i.e.*, a *sounding* of trumpets—sometimes, perhaps more properly, printed, a *sonnet*. Act iii., sc. 1, " of Henry VI.," Part II., opens with " A Sennet." See also " Henry VIII.," act ii., sc. 4, which begins, " Trumpets Sennet, and Cornets."

Page 53, line 7, Two *Gentlewomen*, bearing up her train.] In edit. 1632, " two *Gentlemen*" are represented as bearing up the Queen's train ; but in the edit. 1605, which we follow when not otherwise stated, it stands " two *Gentlewomen*."—" The Queen takes state," at the end of this long introductory stage-direction, means that she ascends her throne, or what had been provided for the purpose.

Page 54, line 4, Whom have you now to *practise* your strictness on ?] This is, we believe, the only word we have had occasion to alter, in this play, in a manner not warranted by any old copy we have had an opportunity of examining : they all read—

" Who have you now to *patronize* your strictness on ?"

But the sense required the change, and the misprint can easily be accounted for. For the sake of the metre, we ought also to leave out " your ;" and we have little doubt that the author so wrote the line.

Page 54, line 9, All your good deeds we'll *quit*, all wrongs remit.] Here we have " quit" in its more ordinary sense of *requite*. See page 38, line 19.   Edit. 1632 has, "your wrongs remit," but the older reading of 1605 is, on all accounts, preferable.

Page 54, line 21, I, Sergeant Trumpeter, present my mace.]   In edit. 1605, this speech wants a prefix, which is derived from later impressions.

Page 54, line 29, Before you let that Purse and Mace be borne.]   It seems doubtful to whom the Queen addresses this and the three preceding lines.   Sir Nicholas Bacon was not made Keeper of the Great Seal till December 22, 1558 : on the second day of her reign, (November 18, 1558) Elizabeth had taken it from Archbishop Heath, having thus early determined that he should not continue in office, although he was made one of her Privy Council.   "The Purse and Mace" spoken of in the line we have quoted, might be the insignia of the Lord Chamberlain, but Lord Hunsdon was not appointed to that office until afterwards : Lord Howard of Effingham first filled that post, according to Camden's Elizabeth.— Kennett, ii , 369.

Page 54, line 32, *Sennet* about the stage in order.]   *i.e.*, *Sound* about the stage in order.   See note to page 53, line 1.

Page 55, line 1, This purse and Bible to your Majesty.]   Stow says— " The 19th of November, Queen Elizabeth came from Bishop's Hatfield, in Hertfordshire, unto the Lord North's house, in the late dissolved Charter-house of London, the Sheriffs of London meeting her grace at the farther end of Barnet town, within the shire of Middlesex, and so rode before her, till she came to the Charter-house gate, next Aldersgate, where her grace remained."   He tells us nothing about the Lord Mayor, the purse, and the Bible; but see the Introduction.

THE

SECOND PART OF

IF YOU KNOW NOT ME,

YOU KNOW NO BODIE.

With the building of the Royall
EXCHANGE :

And the famous Victorie of Queene *Elizabeth*,
in the Yeare 1588.

DRAMATIS PERSONÆ.

Earl of LEICESTER.
Earl of SUSSEX.
Lord HUNSDON.
Sir ANTHONY BROWN.
Sir FRANCIS DRAKE.
Sir MARTIN FROBISHER.
CASSIMIR, and other Ambassadors.
Sir THOMAS GRESHAM.
JOHN GRESHAM, his Nephew.
HOBSON, a Haberdasher.
TIMOTHY, his Man.
JOHN GOODFELLOW, a Pedlar.
Sir THOMAS RAMSEY.
Dr. NOWELL, Dean of St. Paul's.
Dr. PARRY.
HONESTY and QUICK.
Clown.
Lord Mayor, Sheriffs, Sword-bearer, &c.
Chorus.
Duke of MEDINA, DON PEDRO, JOHN MARTINUS RICALDUS,
    and other Spaniards.

Queen ELIZABETH.
Lady RAMSEY.
French Courtesan.
Factors, Apprentices, Merchant, Jeweller, Interpreter, Pursuivant,
    Mariner, Workmen, Boy, Waits, Girl, Lords, Courtiers, Cre-
    ditors, Posts, &c.

IF YOU KNOW NOT ME, YOU KNOW NOBODY.

THE SECOND PART.

WITH

THE BUILDING OF THE EXCHANGE.

ACTUS PRIMUS. SCÆNA PRIMA.

Enter one of Gresham's *Factors, and a Barbary Merchant.*

Fact. My master, sir, requests your company,
About confirming certain covenants
Touching your last night's conference.

Mer. The sugars.
Believe me, to his credit be it spoke,
He is a man of heedful providence,
And one that by innative courtesy
Wins love from strangers. Be it without offence,
How are his present fortunes reckoned?

Fact. Neither to flatter, nor detract from him,
He is a merchant of good estimate :
Care how to get, and forecast to increase,
(If so they be accounted) be his faults.

Mer. They are special virtues, being clear
From avarice and base extortion.
But here he comes.

Enter GRESHAM.

      Good day to Master Gresham.
You keep your word.
 Gresh. Else should I ill deserve
The title that I wear: a merchant's tongue
Should not strike false.
 Mer. What think you of my proffer
Touching the sugar?
 Gresh. I bethought myself
Both of the gain and losses incident,
. And this, I take't, was the whole circumstance.
It was my motion, and, I think, your promise,
To get me a seal'd patent from your king,
For all your Barbary sugar, at a price,
During the king's life; and for his princely love,
I am to send him three score thousand pounds.
 Mer. 'Twas so condition'd, and to that effect
His highness' promise is already past;
And if you dare give credit to my trust,
Send but your private letters to your factor,
That deals for your affairs in Barbary,
His majesty shall either seal your patent,
Or I'll return the money to your factor.
 Gresh. As much as I desire. Pray, sir, draw near,
And taste a cup of wine, whilst I consider,
And thoroughly scan such accidental doubts
As may concern a matter of such moment.
 Mer. At your best leisure.   [*Exit.*
 Gresh. I'll resolve you straight.—
Bethink thee, Gresham, three score thousand pounds;
A good round sum: let not the hope of gain
Draw thee to loss. I am to have a patent
For all the Barbary sugars, at a rate.
The gain clears half in half; but then the hazard.

My term continues during the king's life:
The king may die before my first return;
Then where's my cash?   Why, so the king may live
These forty years; then, where is Gresham's gain?
It stands in this, as in all ventures else,
Doubtful. No more; I'll through, whate'er it cost,
So much clear gain, or so much coin clear lost.—
Within there, ho!

    Enter JOHN GRESHAM.   *Two or three Factors.*

    1st Fact. At hand, sir: did you call?
    Gresh. How thrives our cash?   What, is it well
       increas'd?
I speak like one that must be forc'd to borrow.
    1st Fact. Your worship's merry.
    Gresh. Merry?   Tell me, knave,
Dost thou not think that three score thousand pounds
Would make an honest merchant try his friends?
    1st Fact. Yes, by my faith, sir; but you have a friend
Would not see you stand out for twice the sum.
    Gresh. Praise God for all.   But what's the common
       rumour
Touching my bargain with the King of Barbary?
    1st Fact. 'Tis held your credit and your country's
       honour,
That, being but a merchant of the city,
And taken, in a manner, unprovided,
You should, upon a mere presumption
And naked promise, part with so much cash,
Which the best merchants both in Spain and France
Denied to venture on.
    Gresh. Good; but withal,
What do they think in general of the bargain?
    1st Fact. That if the king confirm and seal your patent,
London will yield you partners enow.

Gresh. I think no less.—Go, fit you for the sea:
I mean to send you into Barbary,
You into Venice, you to Portingal.
Provide you presently.—Where much is spent,
Some must be got: thrift should be provident.—
Come hither, cousin: all the rest depart.

[Exeunt Factors.

John. I had as good depart, too; for he'll ring a peal
    in mine ear,
'Twill sound worse than a passing-bell.

Gresh. I have ta'en note of your bad husbandry,
Careless respect, and prodigal expense,
And out of my experience counsel you.

John. And I hope, good uncle, you think I am as
ready to take good counsel, as you to give it; and I
doubt not but to clear myself of all objections that foul-
mouthed envy shall intimate against me.

Gresh. How can you satisfy the great complaint
Preferr'd against you by old Mistress Blunt,
A woman of approved honesty?

John. That's true; her honesty hath been proved
ofter than once or twice. But do you know her, uncle?
are you inward with her course of life? She's a common midwife for trade-fallen virginity: there are more
maidenheads charged and discharged in her house in a
year, than pieces at the Artillery-yard.

Gresh. She brings in farther proof that you miscall'd her.

John. I never call'd her out of her name, by this
hand, uncle, to my remembrance.

Gresh. No? she says you call'd her bawd.

John. True; and I have known her answer to't a
thousand times. Tut, uncle; 'tis her name, and I know
who gave it her, too: by the same token, her godfather
gave her a bowed angel, standing at the door, which
she hath kept time out of mind.

Gresh. Antonio reports you love his wife.

John. Love? why, alas, uncle, I hold it a parcel of my duty to love my neighbours; and should I hate his wife, no man would hold me a fit member for a commonwealth.

Gresh. He hates you for't.

John. Why, alas, uncle, that's not my fault; I'll love him ne'er the less. You know we are commanded to love our enemies; and, though he would see me hang'd, yet will I love his wife.

Gresh. He told me, you bestowed a gown of a strumpet.

John. Why, alas, uncle, the poor whore went naked; and you know the text commands us to clothe the naked; and [if] deeds of mercy be imputed unto us for faults, God help the elect!

Gresh. Well, if your prodigal expenses be aim'd
At any virtuous and religious end,
'Tis the more tolerable; and I am proud
You can so probably excuse yourself.

John. Well, uncle, to approve my words, as, indeed, good words without deeds are like your green fig-tree without fruit, I have sworn myself to a more conformable and strict course of life.

Gresh. Well, cousin, hoping you'll prove a new man——

John. A new man! what else, uncle? I'll be a new man from the top to the toe, or I'll want of my will. Instead of tennis-court, my morning exercise shall be at Saint Antlin's: I'll leave ordinaries; and to the end I may forswear dicing and drabbing, keep me more short, uncle. Only allow me good apparel; good rags, I'll stand to't, are better than seven years' 'prenticeship, for they'll make a man free of any, nay, of all companies, without indenture, father's copy, or any help what-

soever. But I see my error; wild youth must be bridled.
Keep me short, good uncle.

Gresh. On these presumptions I'll apparel thee;
And to confirm this resolution,
I will prefer you unto Master Hobson,
A man of well known discretion.

John. Any thing, good uncle. I have serv'd my
'prenticeship already, but bind me again, and I shall be
content; and 'tis but reason, neither. Send me to the
conduit with the water-tankard: I'll beat linen-bucks,
or any thing, to redeem my negligence.

Gresh. Your education challenges more respect.
The factor dealt for him in France is dead.

John. And you intend to send me in his room.

Gresh. I do, indeed.

John. It is well done, uncle; and 'twill not be amiss
in policy to do so. The only way to curb a dissolute
youth, as I am, is to send him from his acquaintance;
and therefore send me far enough, good uncle: send
me into France, and spare not; and if that reclaim me
not, give me o'er, as past all goodness.

Gresh. Now, afore God, my thoughts were much
          against him,
And my intent was to have chid him roundly;
But his submissive recantation
Hath made me friends with him.—Come, follow me:
I'll do thee good, and that immediately.   [*Exit.*

John. Thank you, good uncle. You'll send me into
France; all for boon; and I do not show you the right
trick of a cousin afore I leave England, I'll give you
leave to call me cut, and cozen me of my patrimony, as
you have done.   [*Exit.*

Enter HOBSON's *'Prentices, and a Boy.*

1st Pren. Prithee, fellow Goodman, set forth the

ware, and look to the shop a little. I'll but drink a
cup of wine with a customer at the Rose and Crown, in
the Poultry, and come again presently.

2nd Pren. I must needs step to the Dagger, in Cheap,
to send a letter into the country unto my father. Stand
by; you are the youngest 'prentice, look you to the shop.
                                            [*Exeunt.*

Enter HOBSON.

Hob. Where be these varlets? Bones o' me, at
    tavern?
Knaves, villains, spend goods! Why, my customers
Must either serve themselves, or pack unserved.
Now they peep, like Italian pantaloons,
Behind an arras; but I'll start you, knaves.
I have a shoeing-horn to draw on your liquor:
What say you to a piece of a salt-eel?
Come forth, you hang-dogs! Bones o' me, the knaves
Fleer in my face! they know me too well.
I talk and prate, and lay't not on their jacks,
And the proud Jacks care not a fig for me;
But, bones a me, I'll turn another leaf.—

Re-enter 'Prentices.

Where have you been, sir?

1st Pren. An honest customer
Requested me to drink a pint of wine.

Hob. Bones a me, must your crimson throat
Be scour'd with wine? your master's glad of beer:
But you'll die bankrupts, knaves and bankrupts all.—
And where have you been?

2nd Pren. At breakfast with a Dagger-pie, sir.

Hob. A Dagger-pie? uds, dagger's, death! these knaves
Sit cock-a-hoop, but Hobson pays for all.
But, bones a me, knaves, either mend your manners,
Leave ale-houses, taverns, and the tippling mates,

Your punks and cockatrices, or I'll clap ye
Close up in Bridewell: bones a me, I'll do't.

2nd Pren. Beseech you, sir, pardon this first offence.

Hob. First? bones a me, why, 'tis your common course.
And you must needs be guzzling, go by turns,
One to the ale-house, and two keep the shop.

Enter Pedlar with tawney coat.

2nd Pren. It shall be done, sir.—How much ware
would you have?

Taw. Five pounds' worth, in such commodities
As I bespoke last night.

1st Pren. They are ready sorted.

Taw. God bless you, Master Hobson.

Hob. Bones a me, knave, thou'rt welcome. What's
        the news
At bawdy Barnwell, and at Stourbridge fair?
What, have your London wenches any trading?

Taw. After the old sort, sir: they visit the Tolbooth
and the Bull-ring still.

Hob. Good girls! they do their kind. What, your
        pack's empty?
Good news, a sign you bring your purses full;
And, bones a me, full purses must be welcome.—
Sort out their wares.—Welcome's your due;
Pay the old debt, and pen and ink for new.

Taw. We have for you, sir, as white as bears' teeth.

Hob. Bones a God, knaves!—You are welcome; but
        what news?
What news i' th' country? what commodities
Are most respected with your country girls?

Taw. 'Faith, sir, our country girls are akin to your
London courtiers; every month sick of a new fashion.
The horning-busk and silken bride-laces are in good
request with the parson's wife: your huge poking-stick

and French periwig, with chambermaids and waiting
gentlewomen. Now, your Puritan's poker is not so huge,
but somewhat longer; a long, slender poking-stick is the
all in all with your Suffolk Puritan. Your silk band, half
farthingales, and changeable fore parts are common;
not a wench of thirteen but wears a changeable fore part

Hob. An ancient wearing: there's some changeable
        stuff
Has been a wear with women time out of mind.

Taw. Besides, sir, many of our young married men
have ta'en an order to wear yellow garters, points, and
shoe-tyings; and 'tis thought yellow will grow a custom.

Hob. 'T has been us'd long at London.

Taw. And 'tis thought 'twill come in request in the
country, too: 'tis a fashion that three or four young
wenches have promised me their husbands shall wear,
or they'll miss of their marks. Then, your mask, silk
lace, washed gloves, carnation girdles, and busk point
suitable, as common as coals from Newcastle: you shall
not have a kitchen-maid scrape trenchers without her
washed gloves; a dairy wench will not ride to market,
to sell her butter-milk, without her mask and her busk.

Hob. Still a good hearing. Let the country pay
Well for their pride; 'tis *gratis* here in London,
And that's the cause 'tis grown so general.
But feed their humours, and do not spare ;
Bring country money for our London ware.

                                    [*Exit Pedlar.*

        Enter GRESHAM *and* JOHN GRESHAM.

Gresh. Where's Master Hobson?—Cry you mercy, sir.
Hob. No harm, good Master Gresham; pray draw
        near.
I'll but despatch a few old customers,
And bend a present ear to your discourse.

Gresh. At your best leisure.—

Hob. My task is done.

Oh! Master Gresham, 'twas a golden world,

When we were boys: an honest country yeoman,

Such as our fathers were, Heaven rest their souls,

Would wear white kersey.—Bones a me, you knaves!

Stools for these gentlemen.—Your worship's welcome.

Gresh. You know my business.

Hob. About your kinsman:

He shall be welcome. Beseech you, gentlemen,

Less of your courtesy. When shall we see the youth?

Gresh. Why, this is he.

Hob. Which, bones a me, which?

Gresh. Why, this.

Hob. Which? where? What, this young gentleman?

Bones a me, man, he's not for Hobson's turn.

He looks more like my master than my servant.

Gresh. I must confess, he is a gentleman,

And my near kinsman: were he mine own child,

His service should be yours.

Hob. I thank you for't;

And for your sake, I'll give him entertainment.

But, gentleman, if you become my man,

You must become more civil: bones a me,

What a curl'd pate is here! I must ha't off.

You see my livery: Hobson's men are known

By their frieze coats. An you will dwell with me,

You must be plain, and leave off bravery.

John. I hope, sir, to put on such civil conformity, as

you shall not repent my entertainment.

Hob. Pray God it prove so.

Gresh. If he do respect

An uncle's love, let him be diligent.

Hob. Well, Master Gresham, partly for your love,

And chiefly to supply my present want,

Because you say your kinsman is well seen
Both in languages and factorship,
I do intend to send him into France,
In trust both with my merchandizes and my cash.

John. And if I take not order to cashier that and
myself, too, a pox of all French farthingales.

Gresh. How stand you minded to your master's
motion?

John. Somewhat unwilling to leave my acquaintance;
but, good uncle, I know you send me out of love, and I
hope 'twill be a means to call me home the sooner.

Gresh. Pray God it may.

John. I'll want of my will, else. I'll play a merchant's
part with you, I'll take up French commodities, velvet
kirtles, and taffeta fore parts. I'll have that I go for,
or I'll make half the hot-houses in Dieppe smoke for
this trick.

Hob. What, are your books made even with your
accounts?

1st Pren. I have compar'd our wares with our receipt,
And find, sir, ten pounds difference.

Hob. Bones a me, knave,
Ten pounds in a morning? here's the fruit
Of Dagger-pies and ale-house guzzlings.
Make even your reckonings, or, bones a me, knaves,
You shall all smart for't.

2nd Pren. Hark you, fellow Goodman:
Who took the ten pounds of the country chapman,
That told my master the new fashions?

1st Pren. Fore God, not I.

3rd Pren. Not I.

Hob. Bones a me, knaves,
I have paid soundly for my country news.
What was his name?

1st Pren. Afore God, I know not.

2nd Pren. I never saw him in the shop till now.

Hob. Now, bones a me, what careless knaves keep I!
Give me the book. What habit did he wear?

1st Pren. As I remember me, a tawney coat.

Hob. Art sure? then, set him down John Tawney-
  coat.

1st Pren. Ten pound in trust unto John Tawney-
coat.

Hob. Bones a me, man, these knaves will beggar me.

Gresh. By'r lady, sir, ten pounds is too much to lose;
But ten times ten pound cannot shake your credit.

Hob. Thank God for all: when I came first to town,
It would have shook me shrewdly. But, Master Gresham,
How stands your difference with Sir Thomas Ramsey?
Are you made friends yet?

Gresh. He is so obstinate,
That neither juries nor commissions,
Nor the entreaties of his nearest friends,
Can stoop him unto composition.

Hob. 'Tis passing strange. Were Hobson in your
  coat,
Ere I'd consume a penny amongst lawyers,
I'd give't poor people; bones a me, I would.

Gresh. A good resolve; but Sir Thomas Ramsey's
  mind
Is of another temper, and ere Gresham
Will give away a tittle of his right,
The law shall beggar me.

Hob. Bones a me, man, 'twill do that quickly.

Gresh. To prevent which course,
The Lady Ramsey hath by earnest suit
Procur'd the reverend preacher, Doctor Nowell,
A man well reckon'd for his grave respect,
To compromise and end our difference.
The place, the Lombard; ten of the clock, the hour

Appointed for the hearing of our cause.
Shall I request your friendly company?

Hob. With all my heart, both company and purse.
Bones a me, knaves, look better to my shop:
Men of our trade must wear good husband's eyes;
'Mongst many chapmen, there are few that buys.—
My leisure now your business attends;
Time's won, not lost, that's spent to make men friends.

[Exeunt omnes.

Enter Doctor NOWELL *and my Lady* RAMSEY.

Lady. Good Master Doctor Nowell, let your love
Now show itself unto me.   Such as they,
Men of the chiefest note within this city,
To be at such a jar doth make me blush,
Whom it doth scarce concern: you are a good man;
Take you the cause in hand, and make them friends:
'Twill be a good day's work, if so it ends.

Dr. Now. My Lady Ramsey, I have heard, ere this,
Of their contentions, their long suit in law;
How by good friends they have been persuaded both,
Yet both but deaf to fair persuasion.
What good will my word do with headstrong men?
Breath, blown against the wind, returns again.

Lady R. Although to gentlemen and citizens
They have been so rash, yet to so grave a man,
Of whom none speak, but speak with reverence,
Whose words are gather'd in by every ear,
As flowers receive the dew that comforts them,
They will be more attentive.   Pray, take it in hand:
'Tis a good deed; 'twill with your virtue stand.

Dr. Now. To be a make-peace doth become me well,
The charitable motion good in you;
And, in good sooth, 'twill make me wet mine eyes
To see them even, have been so long at odds,

And by my means.   I'll do the best I can,
But God must bless my words, for man's but man.

    Lady R. I thank you heartily, and by the hour I know
They will be presently here on the Lombard,
Whither I drew you for this intent:
And see, Sir Thomas is come; pray break with him.

Enter Sir Thomas RAMSEY.

    Dr. Now. Good day to Sir Thomas Ramsey.
    Ram. Master Dean of Paul's, as much to you.
'Tis strange to see you here in Lombard Street,
This place of traffic, whereon merchants meet.
    Dr. Now. 'Tis not my custom: but Sir Thomas——

Enter GRESHAM *and old* HOBSON.

    Hob. Come, come.
Now, body a me! I swear not every day,
You are too too much to blame: two citizens
Such as yourself and Sir Thomas Ramsey are,
To beat yourselves in law six or seven year,
Make lawyers, 'tornies' clerks, and knaves, to spend
Your money in a brabbling controversy,
Even like two fools.   See where the other is,
With our Dean of Paul's.—Ne'er better met;
We two as umpires will conclude a strife
Before the clock strike twelve, that now is eleven,
Lawyers this full seven years have brabbled in,
And with a cup or two of merry-go-down
Make them shake hands. Is't not well said, Master Dean?
    Dr. Now. And I could wish it as well done, Master
        Hobson.
    Gresh. I'll have you both know, though you are my
        friends,
I scorn my cause should stoop or yield to him,
Although he be reputed Ramsey the rich.

Ram. And Gresham shall perceive that Ramsey's
    purse
Shall make him spend the wealth of Osterley,
But he shall know.

Gresh. Know! What shall I know?

Ram. That Ramsey is as good a man as Gresham.

Gresh. And Gresham is as good a man as Ramsey.

Ram. Tut, tut, tut!

Gresh. Tut in thy teeth, although thou art a knight.

Hob. Bones a me, you are both to blame.
We two, like friends, come to conclude your strife,
And you, like fish-wives, fall a-scolding here.

Dr. Now. How stands the difference 'twixt you, my
    good friends?

Lady R. The impatience both of the one and other
Will not permit to hear each other speak.
I'll tell the cause for both; and thus it is.
There is a lordship, called Osterley,
That Master Gresham hath both bought and built upon.

Gresh. And 'tis a goodly manor, Master Dean.

Lady R. Which Osterley, before he dealt therein,
Sir Thomas, my husband here, did think to buy,
And had given earnest for it.

Ram. Then, Gresham, here, deals with the land-seller,
And buys my bargain most dishonestly.

Gresh. God for thy mercy! touch mine honesty?
Away with compromise, with taking up;
The law shall try my cause and honesty.

Ram. 'Twill prove no better than it should, Gresham.

Gresh. 'Twill prove as good as Ramsey's, Ramsey.

Ram. Do not I know thy rising?

Gresh. Ay, and I know thine.

Ram. Why, mine was honestly.

Gresh. And so was mine.

Hob. Heyday! bones a me,

Was't ever seen two men to scold before?
Here's, I know thy rising, and I know thine,
When as God's blessing that hath rais'd them both.
Am I worse because in Edward's days,
When popery went down, I did engross
Most of the beads that were within the kingdom,
That when Queen Mary had renew'd that Church,
They that would pray on beads were forc'd to me?
I made them stretch their purse-strings, grew rich
    thereby;
Beads were to me a good commodity.
   Gresh. No matter for your beads, my right's my right.
   Ram. Yet Gresham shall well know he hath done
    me wrong.
   Gresh. There's law enough to right you: take your
    course.
   Dr. Now. Reason being made man's guide, why is't
    that force
And violent passions do sweep the soul
Into such headlong mischiefs? 'tis only this;
Reason would rule, Nature a rebel is.
You know the fire of your contention
Hath only cherishing, and is maintain'd
From vile affections, whose strength's but thus.
As sultry heat doth make us shun the fire,
An extreme cold doth alter that desire,
All things that have beginnings have their ends:
Your hate must have conclusion; then, be friends.
   Hob. Friends.—Master Doctor Nowell, look you here,
Here's Mr. Gresham's hand.
   Lady R. I'll bring the other.
   Hob. This seven year they have been in law together.
How much such men as they in seven years spend,
Lawyers may laugh at, but let wise men judge.
   Gresh. Friend Hobson.

Ram. Wife, lady.

Hob. Bones a me, I'll hold you fast :
I will not have a couple of such men
Make cackling lawyers rich, and themselves fools,
And for a trifling cause, as I'm old Hobson.

    Gresh. Sir Thomas Ramsey.

    Ram. Master Gresham.

    Hob. Body of me, both shall be school'd.   Master
       Dr. Nowell,
You know the cause, that this contention
Is only that he bought a piece of land,
This had given earnest for; all Adam's earth,
And Adam's earth is free for Adam's sons,
And 'tis a shame men should contend for it.
Whate'er you speak shall for a sentence stand,
And being spoke, they shall shake hand in hand.

    Dr. Now. If I must, then, decide the difference,
Thus shall it be : because that Sir Thomas Ramsey
Has earnest given before you bought the land,
Though you were not acquainted with so much,
I do award he have an hundred pound
Towards his charges ; and for that you
Have both paid for the land and built upon it,
It shall continue yours.   The money you have spent,
Either account it lost, or badly lent.

    Gresh. God's precious ! I have spent five hundred
       pound.

    Ram. And so have I.

    Hob. No matter,
The judgment stands, only this verdict too :
Had you before the law foreseen the loss,
You had not now come home by weeping cross.
Strifes may as well have end 'twixt honest men ;
Lawyers set fools to law, then laugh at them.

    Gresh. Fore God, 'tis true ; and now I think upon it,

We might at first have ended it by friends,
And made ourselves merry with the money.
But being done, 'tis done; then, Sir Thomas Ramsey,
Let's leave both losers: 'tis but a thousand pound;
And if you be as well content as I,
Here we'll shake hands and let our anger die.

    Hob. Shake hands; by the Mary God, Sir Thomas,
      what else?

    Ram. You show yourselves our friends, to make us
      friends;
Then, in good sooth, I'll not be obstinate.

    Lady R. Nay, Master Dr. Nowell, join their hands.
I know the reverend regard of you
Hath temper'd both their hearts.

    Gresh. Madam, 'tis true:
I think to any but so good a man
We should have both been headstrong; but come.

    Dr. Now. With all my heart. Long may you live
      together,
As friend should be to friend, brother to brother.

    Gresh. Amen, amen, Sir Thomas.

    Ram. Amen, amen, Master Gresham.

    Hob. Amen, amen, to you both.
And is this not better than every term
To trot after lawyers?

    Gresh. Good sooth, 'tis true, if we could think it so;
But 'tis man's nature, he desires his woe.— [*A storm.*
Now, passion a me, Sir Thomas, a cruel storm;
An we stay long, we shall be wet to th' skin.
I do not like 't: nay; and it angers me,
That such a famous city as this is,
Wherein so many gallant merchants are,
Have not a place to meet in, but in this,
Where every show'r of rain must trouble them.
I cannot tell, but if I live.—Let's step to the Pope's head;

We shall be dropping dry if we stay here.—
I'll have a mansion built, and such a roof,
That merchants and their wives, friend and their friends,
Shall walk underneath it, as now in Paul's.—
What day of the month is this?

   Hob. Day, Master Gresham? let me see;
I took a fellow's word for twenty pound:
The tenth of March, the tenth of March.

   Gresh. The tenth of March; well, if I live,
I'll raise a work shall make our merchants say,
'Twas a good show'r that fell upon that day.—
How now, Jack?

Enter JOHN GRESHAM.

   John. Sir, my master, here, having prefer'd me to be
his factor into France, I am come to take my leave of you.

   Gresh. I thank him for his care of thee.—Mr. Hobson,
My kinsman's come to take his leave of me;
He tells me you are sending him for France.

   Hob. Bones a me, knave, art there yet?
I thought thou had'st been half way there by this.

   John. I did but stay to take my leave of my uncle.

   Gresh. Oh, Master Hobson, he comes in a very good
     time.
I was bethinking me whom I might send
To fetch this hundred pound I am set to pay
To Sir Thomas Ramsey.   Nay, as we are friends,
We'll have all covenants kept before we part.

   John. God grant that I may see it.

   Gresh. Here, John, take this seal ring:
Bid Timothy presently send me a hundred pound.

   John. Ay, sir.

   Gresh. I am sure he hath it ready told for thee.
We'll stay here, on the Lombard, till thou com'st.

   John. Yes, sir.

Dr. Now. Nay, stay, good John: thou know'st my
    dwelling, John?

John. In Paul's Churchyard, sir.

Dr. Now. The hundred pound thou art sent for bring
    it thither.

John. Yes, marry will I, sir.   *[Exit.*

Dr. Now. And, my good friends, since that so long
    a strife

Hath end by my persuasion, I'll entreat

My house may entertain you for this time;

Where with such necessaries we'll pass the time,

As God shall best be pleas'd, and you contented.

I keep no riot, nor you look for none,

Only my table is for every one.

    Gresh. A cup of sack, and welcome, Master Dean:

Nature is best contented with a mean.   *[Exeunt.*

      Enter TIMOTHY *and* JOHN GRESHAM.

    John. As I told you, Timothy,

You must send my uncle straight a hundred pound:

He dines at Dr. Nowell's, and gave me in charge

To haste with the money after him.

    Tim. You come to me, John, for a hundred pound:
I thank my spiritual maker, I have the the charge of
many hundreds of his now, John. I hope, John, you fear
God.

    John. Fear God? 'sfoot! what else: I fear God and
the devil too.

    Tim. I must tell you, John, and I know it, you have
not fed of the spiritual food, but edified by faith, and
suffered the tares of the wild affections to be burnt.

    John. Foot! thou wouldst not have me make myself a
French martyr, to be burnt at these years, wouldst thou?

    Tim. I have known them, John, of our Church, have
been burnt for other sins before thy years.

John. Ay, by my faith, Timothy, it may be you have; for as close as you carry your teeth together, with "indeed, good brother," I do not think but once in a year a man might find you quartered betwixt the mouth at Bishopgate, and the preaching place in the Spital.

Tim. Now you talk of the Spital, I must say, in very deed, I have been in the Spital.

John. It is more like, Timothy, you have been acquainted with the pox, then.

Tim. But if you should think, John, that I would be there to commit, deal, or, to speak more profanely, to venture in the way of all flesh, you do wrong me, being a brother of the faith.

John. Come, right yourself and your master, then, and send him this one hundred pound. Here's his seal ring; I hope, a warrant sufficient.

Tim. Upon so good security, John, I'll fit me to deliver it.   [*Exit.*

John. Spend it! Heaven send me but once to finger it, and if I do not make a Flanders reckoning on't—and that is, as I have heard mad wags say, receive it here, and revel it away in another place—let me be spit out of the room of good fellowship, and never have so much favour as to touch the skirt of a taffeta petticoat.
Tut, I am young; mine uncle's an old chuff;
And I'll not want, by God, since he hath enough.
I must not let this same wainscot-face, yea and nay, hear me, though.

Re-enter TIMOTHY.

Tim. Here, John; accept my duty to my master. I must tell you, John, I would not have trusted you, John, without so sufficient a discharge.

John. I am the less beholding unto you. But now I have it, because you preach'd to me upon my demand of it, I'll be so bold to lecture to you upon your delivery. Timothy, you know the proverb, good Timothy, that the still sow eats all the draff; and no question the most smooth-tongued fellow, the more arrant knave: God forbid I should call you so, Timothy, yet I will leave this for your further remembrance:—

Under the yea and nay men often buy
Much cozenage, find many a lie:
He that with yea and nay makes all his sayings,
Yet proves a Judas often in his payings,
Shall have this written o'er his grave,
Thy life seem'd pure, yet died a knave.

Tim. Do you hear, John; you know the chapman's word in London, I'll trust you, but no further than I see you. You have the hundred pound, John, but, for that you have wronged us that love to be edified, I will go with you to my master, and see the money delivered.

John. Why, a' trusted me to come with it.

Tim. I care not, by yea and nay: I'll go; by yea and nay, I will.

John. Let me but ask thee this question; whether dost thou go in any love to thy master, or to me?

Tim. Though my master be my master, yet you have stirr'd my stomach.

John. I thought there was the fruit of your puritan patience. Come, let's along, and if I do not show your religion a trick shall be scarce digested with pippins or cheese, let me be called cut. Come along. [*Exeunt.*

Enter HONESTY, *the Serjeant, and* QUICK.

Hon. Fellow Quick, pray thee have a care: if thou canst see John, the upholsterer, I must needs arrest him.

Quick. How much is the debt?

Hon. Some fifty pound.

Quick. Dost thou think he is able to put in bail to the action?

Hon. I think scarce enough.

Quick. Why, then, we'll arrest him, to the Pope's head, call for the best cheer in the house, first feed upon him, and then, if he will not come off, carry him to the Compter. But if he will stretch some four or five pound, being the sum's so great, he shall pass. We'll make him swear he shall not tell he was arrested, and we'll swear to the creditor we cannot meet with him.

Hon. Thou sayest well.

Quick. I have served Scent the perfumer, Tallow the currier, Quarrel the glazier, and some three or four more of our poor smelts, so this morning.

Enter JOHN.

John. I have coursed through two or three lanes, yet the miching slave follows me so close, I cannot give him the slip for this hundred pound. God save me, now 'tis in my hand, I'd rather be hang'd than part from it. Foot! 'twill make a man merry half a year together in France, command wenches, or anything. Part from it, quoth you; that were jest, indeed: shall a young man as I am, and, though I say it, indifferent proper, go into a strange country, and not show himself what metal he is made of, when a comes there? I protest, a very good hundred pound: a hundred pound will go far in France, and when a man hath it not of his own, who should he make bold withal for it, if he may not with his uncle? But see, if that thin-faced rogue be not come again. I must have a trick for him.

Enter TIMOTHY.

Tim. For all your fore-long to and fro, by yea and nay, I'll follow you.

John. Will you? There should be sergeants here-abouts. Will you? Lord, if it be thy will, send me to hit of one, and if I do not show you a trick.—Thou shouldst be a sergeant, by thy peering so.

Hon. Why, Master John, so I am.

John. Thou art happily met; I am looking for one. What's thy name?

Hon. My name, Master John? I have been merry at your uncle's many a time: my name's Honesty.

John. I' faith?

Quick. Nay, I'll assure you his name is Honesty, and I am Quick, his yeoman.

John. Honesty! who, the pox, gave thee that name? But thou must do an office for my uncle.—
Here, Quick, run thou before and enter the action;
There's money: an action of a hundred pound
Against Timothy Thin-beard, Master Gresham's fac-
          tor.—
I hope I shall teach you to dog me.

Quick. An action against Thin-beard: I go.   [*Exit.*

John. Here, Honesty, here's money for thy arrest.
Be sure to take good bail, or clap him fast.—
I hope I shall show you a trick.

Hon. Mum for that.

John. See where he is: God prosper it.
Fasten upon him like a hungry dog upon a piece of
          meat;
And if this be not a trick to catch a fool,
A more knave learn me, and I'll go to school.

Hon. I arrest you, sir.

Tim. Arrest me, thou servant of Satan! at whose
          suit?

Hon. At your master's, Master Gresham's.

Tim. Oh God, for thy mercy! Mr. John, Mr. John!

John. Nay, nay, this hundred pound hath other work
    in hand for me;
You are in the devil's hands, and so agree.   [*Exit.*

Tim. My good friend, now what must become of me?

Hon. Unless we shall to the tavern, and drink till
you can send for bail, you must to the Compter.

Tim. Is there no difference made betwixt the faithful
and the unfaithful?

Hon. Faith, very little in paying of debts; but if
you be so holy, I marvel how you ran so far behindhand
with your master.

Tim. I must confess, I owe my master five hundred
pound. How I came so, it is not fit to lay the sins of
our flesh open to every eye; and you know the saying,
"'tis bad to do evil, but worst to boast of it;" yet He
above knows, that sometimes, as soon as I have come
from Bow Church, I have gone to a bawdy-house.

Hon. Nay, it appears so, that now your master hath
smelt out your knavery.

Tim. Not to commit, in very deed, good friends, but
only to see fashions; or to recreate and stir up our
drowsy appetites.

Re-enter QUICK.

Hon. Well, here comes my fellow Quick, and, unless
you will content us for staying, you must along to the
Compter.

Tim. I hope you think "the labourer is worthy of
his hire." We will stay here at the tavern; and, Quick, I
will content thee to carry a letter to my master, wherein
I will make him a restitution of his five hundred pound
by repentance, and show him the way that my frail
nature hath run into.

Hon. Well, we'll be paid by the hour.

Tim. It will not be amiss, if you buy an hour-glass.
                                       [*Exeunt.*

Enter Doctor NOWELL, GRESHAM, *Sir* THOMAS
    RAMSEY, HOBSON, *Lady* RAMSEY.

Gresh. Come, Master Dr. Nowell, now we have done
Our worst to your good cheer, we'd fain be gone;
Only we stay my kinsman's long return,
To pay this hundred pound to Sir Thomas Ramsey.

Dr. Now. Then, assure you he will be here presently.
In the mean time, I have drawn you to this walk,
A gallery wherein I keep the pictures
Of many charitable citizens,
That having fully satisfied your bodies,
You may by them learn to refresh your souls.

Gresh. Are all these pictures of good citizens?

Dr. Now. They are; and I'll describe to you some of
    their births,
How they bestow'd their lives, and did so live,
The fruits of this life might a better give.

Gresh. You shall gain more in showing this to us,
Than you have shown.

Lady R. Good Master Dean, I pray you show it us.

Dr. Now. This was the picture of Sir John Philpot,
    sometime Mayor.
This man at one time, at his own charge,
Levied ten thousand soldiers, guarded the realm
From the incursions of our enemies,
And in the year a thousand three hundred and eighty,
When Thomas of Woodstock, Thomas Percy, with
    other noblemen,
Were sent to aid the Duke of Brittany,
This said John Philpot furnish'd out four ships
At his own charges, and did release the armour
That the poor soldiers had for victuals pawned.
This man did live when Walworth was Lord Mayor,
That provident, valiant, and learned citizen,

That both attach'd and kill'd the traitor Tyler;
For which good service, Walworth, the Lord Mayor,
This Philpot, and four other Aldermen,
Were knighted in the field.
Thus did he live; and yet, before he died,
Assur'd relief for thirteen poor for ever.

Gresh. By the Mary God, a worthy citizen.
On, good my dean.

Dr. Now. This Sir Richard Whittington, three times
        Mayor,
Son to a knight, and 'prentice to a mercer,
Began the library of Gray-friars in London,
And his executors after him did build
Whittington College, thirteen almshouses for poor men,
Repair'd Saint Bartholomew's, in Smithfield,
Glazed the Guildhall, and built Newgate.

Hob. Bones a me, then, I have heard lies;
For I have heard he was a scullion,
And rais'd himself by venture of a cat.

Dr. Now. They did the more wrong to the gentleman.
This, Sir John Allen, mercer, and Mayor of London,
A man so grave of life, that he was made
A Privy Councillor to King Henry the Eighth.
He gave this city a rich collar of gold,
That by the Mayor succeeding should be worn;
Of which Sir William Laxton was the first,
And is continued even unto this year.
A number more there are, of whose good deeds
This city flourish'd.

Gresh. And we may be ashamed,
For in their deeds we see our own disgrace.
We, that are citizens, are rich as they were,
Behold their charity in every street,
Churches for prayer, almshouses for the poor,
Conduits which bring us water; all which good

We do see, and are reliev'd withal,
And yet we live like beasts, spend time and die,
Leaving no good to be remember'd by.

   Lady R. Among the stories of these blessed men,
So many that enrich your gallery,
There are two women's pictures: what are they?

   Dr. Now. They are two that have deserv'd a memory
Worthy the note of our posterity.
This, Agnes Forster, wife to Sir A. Forster,
That freed a beggar at the grate of Ludgate,
Was after Mayor of this most famous city,
And builded the south side of Ludgate up,
Upon which wall these verses I have read:—
" Devout souls, that pass this way,
For M. Foster, late Mayor, honestly pray,
And Agnes his wife, to God consecrate,
That of pity this house made for Londoners in Lud-gate;
So that for lodging and water here nothing they pay,
As their keepers shall answer at dreadful Doomsday."

   Lady R. Oh, what a charitable deed was this!

   Dr. Now. This, Ave Gibson, who in her husband's
       life,
Being a grocer and a Sheriff of London,
Founded a free school at Ratcliff,
There to instruct three score poor children;
Built fourteen almshouses for fourteen poor,
Leaving for tutors fifty pound a year,
And quarterly for every one a noble.

   Lady R. Why should I not live so, that, being dead,
My name might have a register with theirs.

   Gresh. Why should not all of us, being wealthy men,
And by Heaven's blessing only rais'd, but
Cast in our minds how we might them exceed
In goodly works, helping of them that need.

   Hob. Bones a me, 'tis true: why should we live

To have the poor to curse us, being dead?
Heaven grant that I may live, that, when I die,
Although my children laugh, the poor may cry.

Dr. Now. If you will follow the religious path
That these have beat before you, you shall win Heaven.
Even in the mid-day walks you shall not walk the
    street,
But widows' orisons, lazars' prayers, orphans' thanks,
Will fly into your ears, and with a joyful blush
Make you thank God that you have done for them;
When, otherwise, they'll fill your ears with curses,
Crying, we feed on woe, you are our nurses.
Oh! is't not better that young couples say,
You rais'd us up, than, you were our decay?
And mothers' tongues teach their first born to sing
Of our good deeds, than by the bad to wring?

Hob. No more, Master Dr. Nowell, no more.
I think these words should make a man of flint
To mend his life: how say you, Master Gresham?

Gresh. Fore God, they have started tears into my
    eyes;
And, Master Dr. Nowell, you shall see
The words that you have spoke have wrought effect
    in me.

Lady R. And from these women I will take a way
To guide my life for a more blessed stay.

Dr. Now. Begin, then, whilst you live, lest, being
    dead,
The good you give in charge be never done.
Make your own hands your executors, your eyes over-
    seers,
And have this saying ever in your mind:—
    " Women be forgetful, children be unkind,
    Executors be covetous, and take what they find."

Hob. In my time I have seen many of them.

Gresh. I'll learn them to prevent them whilst I live.
The good I mean to do, these hands shall give.

Enter QUICK.

Quick. The matter you wot of is done.

Gresh. Done, knave! what's done?

Quick. He is in huckster's handling, sir; and here he
commends him unto you.

Gresh. Marry, knave, dost tell me riddles? what's
　　all this?

Quick. A thing will speak his own mind to you,
If you please but to open the lip.

Enter Clown.

Clown. By your leave, gentlemen, I am come to smell
out my master here.—Your kinsman John, sir, your
kinsman John.

Gresh. Oh, he has brought the hundred pound. Where
is he?

Quick. It appears by this the matter is of less weight.

Gresh. What, more papers?
Fellow, what hast thou brought me here? a recantation?

Clown. It may be so, for he appears in a white
sheet.

Quick. Indeed, he seems sorry for his bad life.

Gresh. Bad life! bad life, knave! what means all
　　this?
Master Dr. Nowell, pray read it for me,
And I'll read that my kinsman John hath sent.—
Where is he, knave?

Clown. Your worship's no wiser than you should be,
to keep any of that coat.

Gresh. Knave, thou meanest.

Clown. Knave? I mean, sir, but your kinsman John,
That by this time's well forward on his way.

Gresh. Heyday! what have we here? knavery as
    quick as eels:
We'll more of this.

Clown. You were best let me help you hold it, sir.

Gresh. Why, knave, dost think I cannot hold a paper?

Clown. Help will do no hurt; for if the knavery be
as quick as an eel, it may chance to deceive you.

GRESH. (*reads.*)

  " I am a merchant made by chance,
      And lacking coin to venture,
    Your hundred pound's gone toward France;
      Your factor's in the Compter."

Quick. No, sir; he is yet but in the tavern at Compter-
gate; but he shall soon be in, if you please.

Gresh. Away, knave! let me read on:

  " My father gave me a portion,
      You keep away my due;
    I have paid myself a part to spend:
      Here's a discharge for you."

Precious cool! here's a knave round with me.

Dr. Now. Your factor, Timothy Thinbeard, writes to
    you,
Who, as it seems, is arrested at your suit.

Gresh. How! at my suit?

Dr. Now. And here confesseth, by using bad company
He is run behindhand five hundred pound,
And doth entreat you would be good to him.

Gresh. How! run behindhand five hundred pound,
And by bad company?   Master Dean of Paul's,
He is a fellow seems so pure of life,
I durst have trusted him with all I had.

Dr. Now. Here is so much, under his own hand.

Gresh. Ha! let me see.—Who set you to arrest him?

Quick. Why, your kinsman John, sir; your kinsman
John.

Gresh. Ha, ha! in faith, I smell the knavery, then.
This knave, belike mistrusting of my kinsman,
Would come along to see the money given me:
Mad Jack, having no trick to put him off,
Arrests him with a sergeant, at my suit.
There went my hundred pound away: this Thinbeard,
     then,
Knowing himself to have play'd the knave with me,
And thinking I had arrested him indeed,
Confesseth all his tricks with yea and nay.
So, here's five hundred pound come, one run away.

Hob. Bones a me, Master Gresham, is my man John
gone away with your hundred pound?

     Clown. 'Faith, it appears so, by the acquittance that
        I brought.

     Gresh. No matter, Mr. Hobson: the charge you trust
        him with
I'll see he shall discharge. I know he is wild,
Yet, I must tell you, I'll not see him sunk;
And, afore God, it hath done my heart more good,
The knave had wit to do so mad a trick,
Than if he had profited me twice so much.

     Ram. He ever had the name of mad Jack Gresham.

     Gresh. He's the more like his uncle.—Sir Thomas
        Ramsey,
When I was young, I do remember well,
I was as very a knave as he is now.—
Sirrah, bring Thinbeard hither to me; and, Sir Thomas
        Ramsey,
Your hundred pound I'll see you paid myself.
Ha, ha! mad Jack, grammercy for this slight:
This hundred pounds makes me thy uncle right.

                           [*Exeunt.*

         Enter JOHN *Tawney-coat.*

     Taw. Ay, sure, 'tis in this lane: I turned on the

right hand, coming from the Stocks.   Nay, though there
was master careless, man careless, and all careless, I'll
still be honest John, and scorn to take any man's ware
but I'll pay them for it.   I warrant, they think me an
arrant knave, for going away and not paying; and in
my conscience the master cudgell'd the men, and the men
the master, and all about me; when, as God save me, I
did it innocently.   But, sure, this is the lane: there's the
Windmill; there's the dog's head in the pot; and here's
the friar whipping the nun's arse.   'Tis hereabout, sure.

Enter in the shop two of HOBSON'S *folks, and opening the
shop.*

   1st. Come, fellow Crack, have you sorted up those
     wares?
Mark'd them with 54?   They must be packed up.
   2nd. I have done't an hour ago.   Have you seal'd up
My master's letter to his factor, John Gresham?
It is at Dieppe, in France, to send him matches,
For he must use them at Bristow fair.
   1st. Ay, and the post received it two hours since.
   Taw. Sure, it is here about: the kennel was on my
right hand; and I think, in my conscience, I shall never
have the grace of God and good luck, if I do not pay it.
God's foot, look here! look here! I know this is the
shop, by that same stretch-halter.—Oh, my masters! by
your leave, good fellows.
   1st. You are welcome, sir; you are welcome.
   Taw. Indeed, that's the common saying about London, if men bring money with them.
   1st. Oh, sir, money customers to us are best welcome.
   Taw. You say well; so they should be.   Come, turn
o'er your books: I am come to pay this same ten pound.
   1st. And we are ready to receive money.   What
might we call your name?

Taw. Why, my name is John Goodfellow. I hope I
am not ashamed of my name.

1st. Your kin are the more beholding unto you.—
Fellow Crack, turn o'er the kalendar, and look for John
Goodfellow.

2nd. What comes it to?

Taw. Ten pound.

1st. You will have no more wares with you, will you,
sir?

Taw. Nay, prithee, not too fast: let's pay for the old,
before we talk of any new.

2nd. John Goodfellow?—Fellow Nimblechaps, here's
no such name in all our book.

1st. I think thou art mop-ey'd this morning: give
me the book.   Letter I, letter I, letter I.—When had
you your ware?

Taw. I had it some ten days ago.

1st. Your name's John Goodfellow, you say.—Letter I,
letter I, letter I.—You do not come to mock us, do
you?—Letter I, letter I, letter I.—By this hand, if I
thought you did, I would knock you about the ears,
afore we parted.—Fellow Crack, get me a cudgel ready.
Letter I, letter I, letter L—'Foot! here's no such name
in all our book. Do you hear, fellow? Are you drunk,
this morning, to make us look for moonshine in the
water?

Taw. 'Foot! art not thou drunk, this morning? Canst
not receive the money that's due to thee?   I tell thee,
I had ten pounds' worth of ware here.

1st. And I tell thee, John Goodfellow, here's no such
name in our book, nor no such ware delivered.

Taw. God's precious! there's a jest, indeed : so a
man may be sworn out of himself.—Had I not ten
pounds' worth of ware here?

2nd. No, goodman goose, that you had not.

Taw. Heyday! here's excellent fellows, are able to make their master's hair grow through his hood in a month! They can not only carelessly deliver away his ware, but also they will not take money for it, when it comes.

1st. Do you hear, hoiden? an my master were not in the next room, I'd knock you about th' ears for playing the knave with us, ere you parted.

Taw. By the mass, I think your master had more need (if he look'd well about him) to knock you for playing the Jacks with him. There's your ten pounds; tell it out with a wannion, and take it for your pains.

1st. 'Foot! here's a mad slave, indeed, will give us ten pound, in spite of our teeth.

2nd. Fellow Nimblechaps, alas! let the poor fellow alone: it appears he is beside himself.

Taw. By the mass, I think you will sooner make your master stark mad, if you play thus with everybody.

Enter old HOBSON.

Hob. Heyday! bones a me, here's lazy knaves!
Past eight o'clock, and neither ware sorted,
Nor shop swept.

Taw. Good morrow to you, sir: have you any more stomach to receive money than your men have, this morning?

Hob. Money is welcome chaffer: welcome, good friend, welcome, good friend.

Taw. Here's Monsieur Malapert, your man, scorns to receive it.

Hob. How, knaves! think't scorn to receive my
            money?
Bones a me, grown proud, proud knaves, proud?

1st. I hope we know, sir, you do not use to bring up your servants to receive money, unless it be due unto you.

Hob. No, bones a me, knaves, not for a million.—
Friend, come to pay me money? for what, for what?
For what come you to pay me money?

Taw. Why, sir, for ware I had some month ago,
Being pins, points, and laces,
Poking-sticks for young wives, for young wenches
    glasses,
Ware of all sorts, which I bore at my back,
To sell where I come, with what do you lack?
What do you lack? what do you lack?

Hob. Bones a me, a merry knave. What's thy name?

Taw. My name, sir, is John Goodfellow,
An honest poor pedlar of Kent.

Hob. And had ten pound in ware of me a month ago?
Bones! give me the books. John Goodfellow, of Kent.

Taw. Oh, sir, *nomine et naturâ*, by name and nature.
I am as well known for a good fellow in Kent,
As your city Sumner's known for a knave.
Come, sir, will you be telling?

Hob. Tell me no tellings: bones a me! here's no such
    matter.
Away, knave, away! thou owest me none. Out of my
    doors!

Taw. How! owe you none, say you? This is but a
trick to try my honesty, now.

Hob. There's a groat: go, drink a pint of sack;
Comfort thyself; thou art not well in thy wits.
God forbid, pay me ten pound not due to me?

Taw. God's dickins, here's a jest, indeed! master
mad, men mad, and all mad: here's a mad household.
Do you hear, Master Hobson, I do not greatly care to
take your groat, and I care as little to spend it; yet
you shall know I am John, honest John, and will not be
outfac'd of my honesty. Here I had ten pounds' worth
of ware, and I will pay for it.

Hob. Nimblechaps! call for help, Nimblechaps.

Bones a me, the man begins to rave.

2nd. Master, I have found out one John Tawney-
    coat,

Had ten pounds' worth of ware a month ago.

Taw. Why, that's I, that's I! I was John Tawney-
    coat then,

Though I am John Grey-coat now.

Hob. John Tawney-coat! Welcome, John Tawney-
    coat.

Taw. 'Foot! do you think I'll be outfac'd of my
    honesty?

Hob. A stool for John Tawney-coat.—Sit, good John
    Tawney-coat;

Honest John Tawney-coat, welcome John Tawney-coat.

Taw. Nay, I'll assure you, we were honest, all the
    generation of us.

There 'tis, to a doit, I warrant it: you need not tell it
after me.

'Foot! do you think I'll be outfac'd of mine honesty?

Hob. Thou art honest John, honest John Tawney-coat.

Having so honestly paid for this,

Sort up his pack straight worth twenty pound.

I'll trust thee, honest John; Hobson will trust thee;

And any time the ware that thou dost lack,

Money, or money not, I'll stuff thy pack.

Taw. I thank you, Master Hobson; and this is the
fruit of honesty.

Enter a Pursuivant.

Purs. By your leave, Master Hobson, I bring this
    favour to you.

My royal mistress, Queen Elizabeth,

Hath sent to borrow a hundred pound of you.

Hob. How! bones a me, Queen know Hobson?

    Queen know Hobson,

And send but for one hundred pound? Friend, come in;
Come in, friend; shall have two; Queen shall have two.
If Queen know Hobson once, her Hobson's purse
Must be free for her; she is England's nurse.
Come in, good friend. Ha! Queen know Hobson?
Nay, come in, John; we'll dine together too.

Taw. Make up my pack, and I'll along from you,
Singing merrily on the way,
Points, pins, gloves, and purses,
Poking-sticks, and black jet rings,
Cambrics, lawns, and pretty things.
Come, maids, and buy, my back doth crack,
I have all that you want; what do you lack?
What do you lack?   [*Exeunt.*

Enter GRESHAM *and Sword-bearer.*

Gresh. Our city's sword-bearer, and my very good
            friend,
What, have our honourable Court of Aldermen
Determin'd yet? shall Gresham have a place
To erect this worthy building to his name,
May make the city speak of him for ever?

Sword. They are in earnest council, sir, about it.

Gresh. Be you my agent to and fro to them:
I know your place, and will be thankful to you.
Tell them, I wait here in the Mayor's Court;
Beneath, in the Sheriff's Court, my workmen wait,
In number full an hundred: my frame is ready;
All only stay their pleasure; then, out of hand,
Up goes my work, a credit to the land.

Sword. I shall be dutiful in your request.   [*Exit.*

Gresh. Do, good Master Sword-bearer.—Now, when
This work is rais'd,
It shall be in the pleasure of my life
To come and meet our merchants at their hour,

And see them, in the greatest storm that is,
Walk dry, and in a work I rais'd for them;
Or fetch a turn with[in] my upper walk,
Within which square I have ordered shops shall be
Of neat, but necessariest trades in London:
And in the richest sort being garnish'd out,
'Twill do me good to see shops, with fair wives
Sit to attend the profit of their husbands;
Young maids brought up, young men as 'prentices.
Some shall prove masters, and speak in Gresham's praise,
In Gresham's work we did our fortunes raise;
For I dare say, both country and the Court
For wares shall be beholding to this work.

    Enter Sword-bearer, Lord Mayor, and Sheriffs.

  Sword. Master Gresham,
Thus sends the Lord Mayor and Court of Aldermen.
  Ram. Or rather come to bring the news ourselves.
We have determin'd of a place for you
In Cornhill, the delightful of this city,
Where you shall raise your frame.   The city at their
      charge
Hath bought the houses and the ground,
And paid for both three thousand, five hundred, three
      and twenty pound.
Order is given the houses shall be sold
To any man will buy them, and remove them.
  Sher. Which is already done, being four score house-
      holds,
Were sold at four hundred, three score, and eighteen
      pounds.
The plot is also planed at the city's charges,
And we, in name of the whole citizens,
Do come to give you full possession
Of this, our purchase, whereon to build a Burse,

A place for merchants to assemble in,
At your own charges.

   Gresh. Master Sheriff, I'll do't; and what I spend
     therein,
I scorn to lose day; neglect is a sin.—
Where be my workmen?

Enter Workmen.

   Work. Here, here! with trowel and tools ready at
hand.
Enter Dr. NOWELL *and* HOBSON.

   Gresh. Come, fellows, come:
We have a frame made, and we have room
To raise it.—But, Master Dr. Nowell and Master Hobson,
We have your presence in a happy time:
This seventh of June, we the first stone will lay
Of our new Burse.—Give us some bricks.
Here's a brick, here's a fair sovereign.
Thus I begin; be it hereafter told,
I laid the first stone with a piece of gold.
He that loves Gresham follow him in this:
The gold we lay due to the workmen is.

   Work. Oh, God bless Mr. Gresham! God bless
Mr. Gresham!

   Ram. The Mayor of London, Mr. Gresham, follows
     you.
Unto your first this second I do fit,
And lay this piece of gold o' top of it.

   Sher. So do the Sheriffs of London after you.

   Hob. And, bones a me, old Hobson will be one.
Here, fellows, there's my gold; give me a stone.

   Work. God forbid, a man of your credit should want
stones.

   Dr. Now. Is this the plot, sir, of your work in hand?

   Gresh. The whole plot, both of form and fashion.

Dr. Now. In sooth, it will be a good edifice;
Much art appears in it: in all my time,
I have not seen a work of this neat form.
What is this vaultage for, is fashion'd here?

    Gresh. Stowage for merchants' ware, and strangers'
        goods,
As either by exchange or other ways are vendible.

    Dr. Now. Here's a middle round, and a fair space,
The round is grated, and the space
Seems open: your conceit for that?

    Gresh. The grates give light unto the cellarage,
Upon the which I'll have my friends to walk,
When Heaven gives comfortable rain unto the earth,
For that I will have covered.

    Dr. Now. So it appears.

    Gresh. This space, that hides not heaven from us,
Shall be so still; my reason is,
There's summer's heat as well as winter's cold;
And I allow, and here's my reason for't,
'Tis better to be bleak'd by winter's breath,
Than to be stifled up with summer's heat.
In cold weather, walk dry, and thick together,
And every honest man warm one another:
In summer, then, when too much heat offends,
Take air, a' God's name, merchants or my friends.

    Dr. Now. And what of this part, that is over head?

    Gresh. Master Dean, in this
There is more ware there than in all the rest.
Here, like a parish for good citizens
And their fair wives to dwell in, I'll have shops,
Where every day they shall become themselves
In neat attire; that when our courtiers
Shall come in trains to pace old Gresham's Burse,
They shall have such a girdle of chaste eyes,
And such a globe of beauty round about,

Ladies shall blush to turn their visors off,
And courtiers swear they ly'd when they did scoff.

 Dr. Now. Kind Master Gresham, this same work of
  yours
Will be a tomb for you, after your death;
A benefit to tradesmen, and a place
Where merchants meet, their traffic to maintain,
Where neither cold shall hurt them, heat, nor rain.

 Gresh. Oh, Master Nowell, I did not forget
The troublesome storm we had in Lombard Street,
That time Sir Thomas and I were adversaries,
And you and Master Hobson made us friends.
I then did say, and now I'll keep my word,
I saw a want, and I would help afford:
Nor is my promise, given you when you show'd
That rank of charitable men to us,
That I would follow their good actions,
Forgot with me; but that before I die
The world shall see I'll leave like memory.

       [*A blazing star.*

Fore God, my lord, have you beheld the like?
Look how it streaks! what do you think of it?

 Sher. 'Tis a strange comet.—Master Hobson,
My time, to my remembrance, hath not seen
A sight so wonderful.—Master Dr. Nowell,
To judge of these things your experience
Exceedeth ours; what do you hold of it?
For I have heard that meteors in the air,
Of lesser form, less wonderful than these,
Rather foretel of dangers imminent,
Than flatter us with future happiness.

 Dr. Now. Art may discourse of these things; none
  can judge
Directly of the will of Heaven in this:
And by discourse thus far I hold of it.

That this strange star appearing in the North,
And in the constellation of Cassiopy,
Which, with three fixed stars commix'd to it,
Doth make a figure geometrical,
Lozenge-wise, called of the learned rhombus,
Conducted with the hourly moon of Heaven,
And never altered from the fixed sphere,
Foretels such alteration, that, my friends,
Heaven grant with this first sight our sorrow ends.

 Hob. God's will be done. Master Dean, hap what hap will,
Death doth not fear the good man, but the ill.

 Gresh. Well said, Master Hobson:
Let's live to-day, that if death come to-morrow,
He's rather messenger of joy than sorrow.

Enter a Factor.

Now, sir, what news from Barbary?

 Fact. Unwelcome news, sirs. The King of Barbary is slain.

 Gresh. Ha! slain by treason, or by war?

 Fact. By war, in that renowned battle
Swift fame desires to carry through the world,
The battle of Alcazar, wherein two kings,
Besides the King of Barbary, were slain,
Kings of Morocco and of Portingal,
With Stukeley, that renowned Englishman,
That had a spirit equal with a king,
Made fellow with these kings in warlike strife,
Honour'd his country, and concluded life.

 Gresh. Cold news, by'r Lady.—The venture, gentlemen,
Of three score thousand pound with that dead king,
Lies in a hazard to be won or lost.
In what estate consists the kingdom now?

Fact. In peace ; and the succeeding happy heir
Was crown'd then king, when I took ship from
    thence.

Gresh. To that king, then, be messenger from us,
And by the sound of trumpet summon him.
Say that thy master, and a London merchant,
Craves due performance of such covenants,
Confirm'd by the late King unto ourself,
That for the sum of three score pound,
The traffic of his sugars should be mine.
If he refuse the former bargain made,
Then, freely claim the money that we lent :
Say that our coin did stead the former king ;
If he be kind, we have as much for him.

Hob. By the Mary God, it was a dangerous day :
Three kings, besides young Stukeley, slain !
I'll tell you, my Lord Mayor, what I have seen.
When sword and bucklers were in question,
I have seen that Stukeley beat a street before him.
He was so familiar grown in every mouth,
That if it happen'd any fighting were,
The question straight was, was not Stukeley there?
Bones a me, he would hew it !—Now, what news with
    you ?

Enter a boy.

Boy. Here's a letter sent you from John Gresham.

Hob. Oh, an answer of a letter that I sent,
To send me matches against Bristow fair,
If then any were come.

Boy. I cannot tell, sir, well what to call it ; but, instead of matches of ware, when you read your letter, I believe you will find your factor hath match'd you.

Hob. What's here? what's here?   [*Read the letter.*
" As near as I could guess at your meaning, I have

laboured to furnish you, and have sent you two thousand pounds' worth of match."

How? bones, knave! two thousand pounds' worth of
    match!

Boy. Faith, master, never chafe at it; for if you cannot put it away for match, it may be the hangman will buy some of it for halters.

Hob. Bones a me, I sent for matches of ware, fellows
    of ware.

Boy. And match being a kind of ware, I think your factor hath match'd you.

Hob. The blazing star did not appear for nothing.
I sent to be sorted with matches of ware,
And he hath sent me naught but a commodity of match,
And in a time when there's no vent for it.
What do you think on't, gentlemen?
I little thought Jack would have serv'd me so.

Gresh. Nay, Master Hobson, grieve not at Jack's cross;
My doubt is more, and yet I laugh at loss.   [*Exeunt.*

Enter two Lords.

1st Lord. You have travell'd, sir: how do you like
    this building?
Trust me, it is the goodliest thing that I have seen;
England affords none such.

2nd Lord. Nor Christendom;
I might say, all the world has not his fellow.
I have been in Turkey's great Constantinople;
The merchants there meet in a goodly temple,
But have no common Burse: in Rome—but Rome's
Built after the manner of Frankfort and Embden—
There, where the greatest marts and meeting places
Of merchants are, have streets and pent-houses,
And, as I might compare them to themselves,
Like Lombard Street, before this Burse was built.

Enter Sir THOMAS RAMSEY.

1st Lord. I have seen the like in Bristow.

Ram. Good morrow to your honours.

2nd Lord. Thanks to my good Lord Mayor.
We are gazing here of Master Gresham's work.

Ram. I think you have not seen a goodlier frame.

2nd Lord. Not in my life; yet I have been in Venice,
In the Rialto there, called Saint Mark's;
'Tis but a bauble, if compar'd to this.
The nearest, that which most resembles this,
Is the great Burse in Antwerp, yet not comparable
Either in height or wideness, the fair cellarage,
Or goodly shops above. Oh, my Lord Mayor,
This Gresham hath much graced your city, London;
His fame will long outlive him.

1st Lord. It is reported you, Sir Thomas Ramsey,
Are as rich as he: this should incite you
To such noble works, to eternize you.

Ram. Your lordship pleases to be pleasant with me:
I am the meanest of a many men
In this fair city. Master Gresham's fame
Draws me as a spectator amongst others,
To see his cost, but not compare with it.

1st Lord. And it is cost, indeed.

2nd Lord. But when, to fit these empty rooms about
    here,
The pictures graven of all the English kings
Shall be set over, and in order plac'd,
How glorious will it then be!

1st Lord. Admirable!

Ram. These very pictures will surmount my wealth.

1st Lord. But how will Master Gresham name this
    place?

2nd Lord. I heard my Lord of Leicester to the Queen

Highly commend this work; and she then promis'd
To come in person, and here christen it:
It cannot have a better godmother.
This Gresham is a royal citizen.

Ram. He feasts this day the Russian Ambassador:
I am a bidden guest; where, if it please you——

1st Lord. Good Sir Thomas,
We know what you would say.   We are his guests,
Invited too; yet in our way we took
This wonder, worth our pains: it is our way
To Bishopsgate, to Master Gresham's house;
Thither, so please you, we'll associate you.   [*Exeunt.*

Enter GRESHAM, *leading in the Ambassador.   Music,
and a banquet served in: the Ambassador sits.*

Enter Sir THOMAS RAMSEY, *the two Lords, my Lady*
RAMSEY, *the Waits, in Sergeants' gowns, with one Interpreter.*

   Gresh. Lords, all at once, welcome; welcome at
      once.
You come to my new building's up-setting:
It hath been long in labour, now deliver'd,
And up; anon, we'll have a health to it.
This Russian prince, the Emperor's ambassador,
Doth not our language understand.—Interpreter,
Say that we bid him welcome.

   Inter. The Prince speaks Latin,
And in that language we'll interpret for him.
*Salutem tibi optat, et adventum tuum gravissimus
Iste Londinensis.*

   *Amb. Istum libens audio, ages illi meo nomine
Ex animo gratias: funde, quod bibamus.*

   Inter. He gladly thanks you for his royal welcome,
And drinks to you.

   Gresh. We understand that sign.—

Come, let our full-crown'd cups o'erflow with wine.
Welcome again, fair lords.

2nd Lord. Thanks, Master Gresham:
We have been viewing of your works.

Gresh. My Burse: how do you like it, lords?
It is a pretty bauble.

2nd Lord. 'Tis a fair work:
Her Majesty intends to name the place.

Gresh. She doth her servant Gresham too much grace.
It will be pretty when my pictures come
To fill those empty rooms; if that hold,
That ship's rich freight is worth her weight in gold.

1st Lord. It will be rare and famous.

Gresh. What was it that the Russian whispered?

Inter. He ask'd me what interpreter the Queen
Would in his embassy employ.

Gresh. None: tell him none;
For, though a woman, she is a rare linguist.
Where other princes use interpreters,
She, *propriâ voce*,—I have some Latin too—
She of herself hears all their embassies,
And herself answers them without interpreter,
Both Spanish, Latin, French, and Greek,
Dutch, and Italian: so let him know.
My Lord of Leicester sent me word, last night,
(And I am prouder on't than on my building)
The Queen, to grace me and my works the more,
The several Ambassadors there will hear,
And them in person answer.

2nd Lord. 'Tis most true.

Enter a gentleman, whispering to Sir THOMAS RAMSEY.

Gresh. The Russian with the French.—
What would that gentleman, Sir Thomas?

Ram. He is a merchant and a jeweller:

'Mongst other stones, he saith, he hath a pearl,
Orient and round, weighing so many carats,
That it can scarce be valued: the French king
And many other dukes have, for the riches
And price, refused to buy it; now he comes
To offer it to this Ambassador.

Gresh. Show him the pearl, interpreter,
The Lord Ambassador.

*Inter. Mercator quidam et aurifex, spectendum tibi
　　profert*
Gemmam, domine serenissime.

*Amb. Et pulchra, et principe digna : interroga quanti
　　judicat.*

Inter. He commends it to be both rich and fair,
And desires to know how you value it.

Mer. My price, sir, is fifteen hundred pound.

Amb. Quanti valet ?

Inter. Mille quingentis minis.

Amb. Non, non ; nimis percara est ista gemma.

Inter. He saith it is too dear; he will not buy it.

Gresh. I will peruse your pearl.　Is that your price?

Mer. I cannot bate one crown, and gain by it.

Gresh. We'll not be accessary to your loss;
And yet, considering all things, some may think us
To be but bare of treasure at this time,
Having disburs'd so much about our works;

Enter a Mariner.

Yet, if our ships and trade in Barbary
Hold current, we are well.—What news from sea?
How stand my ships?

Mar. Your ships, in which all the king's pictures were,
From Brute unto our Queen Elizabeth,
Drawn in white marble, by a storm at sea
Are wreck'd and lost.

Gresh. The loss, I weigh not this;
Only it grieves me, that my famous building
Shall want so rich and fair an ornament.

Lady R. It touches all the city; for those pictures
Had doubly grac'd this royal edifice.

Ram. Methinks the ship's loss most should trouble you.

Gresh. My ship's but wealth: why, we have wealth.
The pictures were the grace of my new Burse:
So I might them in their true form behold,
I car'd not to have lost their weights in gold.

Enter a Factor.

1st Lord. A noble citizen!

Gresh. Our factor! What good news from Barbary?
What says the king? Speak: didst thou summon him?
Or hast thou brought my three score thousand pound?
Or shall I have the sugars at that rate?
If so, new marble pictures we'll have wrought,
And in a new ship from beyond sea brought.

Fact. The king, that in the regal chair succeeds
The king late dead, I summon'd, and demanded
Either your money tender'd, or the sugars
After the rate propos'd. He denied both;
Alleging, though he was successive heir,
He was not, therefore, either tied to pay
The late king's debts, nor yet to stand unto
Unnecessary bargains: notwithstanding,
To gratify your love, the king hath sent you
As presents, not as satisfaction,
A costly dagger and a pair of slippers;
And there's all for your three score [thousand] pound.

Gresh. By'r lady, a dear bargain.

1st Lord. I fear me, this will plague him. A strange
cross:
How will he take this news? loss upon loss.

2nd Lord. Nay, will it not undo him? doth he not
 wish
His buildings in his purse?·

Gresh. A dagger? that's well:
A pair of slippers?—Come, undo my shoes.
What, sixty thousand pound in sterling money,
And paid me all in slippers?   Then, hautboys, play!
On slippers I'll dance all my care away.
Fit, fit! he had the just length of my foot.—
You may report, lords, when you come to Court,
You Gresham saw a pair of slippers wear,
Cost thirty thousand pound.

 1st Lord. Somewhat too dear.

 Gresh. Nor yet, for all this treasure we have lost,
Repents it us one penny of our cost.

 2nd Lord. As royal in his virtues as his buildings!

 Ram. These losses would have kill'd me.

 Gresh. Jeweller,
Let's see thy pearl.—Go, pound it in a mortar;
Beat it to powder, then return it me:
What dukes and lords, and these ambassadors
Have, even before our face, refus'd to purchase,
As of too high a price to venture on,
Gresham, a London merchant, here will buy.—
What, is it broken small?   Fill us some wine:
Fuller, yet fuller, till the brim o'erflows.
Here sixteen thousand pound at one clap goes.
Instead of sugar, Gresham drinks this pearl
Unto his Queen and mistress: pledge it, lords.
Who ever saw a merchant bravelier fraught,
In dearer slippers, or a richer draught?

 Ram. You are an honour to all English merchants;
As bountiful, as rich and charitable.
As rich, as renowned, as any of all.

 Gresh. I do not this as prodigal of my wealth;

Rather to show how I esteem that loss
Which cannot be regain'd.   A London merchant
Thus treads on a king's present.—Jeweller,
My factor shall deliver you your money.
And, lords, so please you but to see my school
Of the seven learned liberal sciences,
Which I have founded here, near Bishopsgate,
I will conduct you.   I will make it, Lords,
An university within itself,
And give't from my revenues maintenance.
W' are not like those that are not liberal
Till they be by dying; what we mean to give,
We will bestow and see done whilst we live.—
Attendance! come, th' Ambassador, guests, all,
Your welcome's great, albeit your cheer's but small.

[Exeunt.

Enter Tawney-coat, with a spade.

Taw. Hard world, when men dig living out of stones,
As wretched, miserable I am enforc'd.
And yet there lives more pity in the earth,
Than in the flinty bosoms of her children;
For she's content to have her aged breast
Mangled with mattocks, rent and torn with spades,
To give her children and their children bread;
When man, more flinty than her stony ribs
That was their mother, neither by entreats,
Tears, nor complaints, will yield them sustenance.
But 'tis our age's fault; the mightier
Tear living out of us, we out of her.

Enter HOBSON, in his gown and slippers.

Hob. Mother of me, what a thick mist is here!
I walked abroad to take the morning air,
And I am out of knowledge.   Bones a me,

What meads, and what enclosure have we here?
How now, old Hobson! dote in thine old age?
A fool at three score?   Whither wilt thou, wit?
I cross'd the water in my gown and slippers,
To see my rents and buildings of the Bankside,
And I am slipp'd clean out of ken, 'fore God,
A wool gathering.

    Taw. Either mine ear's deceiv'd,
Or I should know that tongue.   'Tis so, indeed!
Each word he speaks makes my torn heart to bleed.

    Hob. Ha, ha! I smile at my own foolery.
Now I remember mine old grandmother
Would talk of fairies and hobgoblins,
That would lead milkmaids over hedge and ditch,
Make them milk their master neighbour's kine;
And, ten to one, this Robin Goodfellow

                     [*Tawney-coat digs.*

Hath led me up and down the madman's maze.
I hear some company; for shame! all whist.
Sit thee down, Hobson, a right man in the mist.

    Taw. 'Tis he.   Alas! when the rough hand of want
Hath cast us down, it loads us with mishaps.
I broke my day with him.   Oh, had that fatal hour
Broken my heart! and, villain that I was,
Never so much as write in my excuse:
And he for that default hath sued my bill,
And with an execution is come down
To seize my household stuff, imprison me,
And turn my wife and children out of doors.
What, shall I fly him?   No; he's pitiful:
Then, with my tears I will importune him.—
God save you, Master Hobson.

    Hob. Hobson! bones a me,
What voice is that?—Art thou a man, a friend?
Tell me if thou be that Will of the Wisp,

That lead'st me this wild morris?   I conjure thee
To leave me to myself.

   Taw. Oh, Master Hobson!
As ever you have been a poor man's friend,
Continue still so: insult not o'er my fortunes.

   Hob. I am in the mist.   What art thou? speak.

   Taw. A debtor of your worship's.

   Hob. A debtor of mine! mother of me, thou liest.
I know thee not, nor do I know this place.
If thou owest me any thing, pay me with thy love;
And if thou be'st acquainted in these woods,
Conduct me to some town or direct road
That leads to London, and I'll here discharge thee
Of debts and duties, and beside impart
Somewhat to cherish thee.

   Taw. What should I think?
He knows me; and, for fear I should escape him,
He would entice me to the officers.—
Oh, Master Hobson! though not for mine own,
Yet for my wife and my poor children's sakes,
If your intent be to imprison me,
Upon my knees I do entreat you spare me.
The goods you trusted me withal I have not wasted
In riot and excess, but my kind heart,
Seeing my helpless neighbours in distress,
By reason of the long and extreme dearth,
Some I reliev'd, some trusted with my goods,
Whose poverty's not able to repay.
Then, bear with me a little; your rich store
Hath sav'd my life, and fed a hundred more.

   Hob. Now, bones a me, another Tawney-coat!
What's thy name, knave?

   Taw. John Goodfellow, sir.

   Hob. Bones a me,
I thought as much.   Art thou not Tawney-coat?

Taw. I am the man whom you call'd Tawney-coat.

Hob. And I the Hobson that will pity thee.
Now, bones a me, what mak'st thou with a spade?

Taw. This spade? alas! 'tis all the wealth I have.
When my poor wife and children cry for bread,
They still must cry till these have purchas'd it;
They must go naked till these harden'd hands,
When the cold breath of winter strikes on them,
Till these have earned it.

Hob. Now, alas, good soul!
It melts my heart to hear him, and mine eyes
Could weep for company.—What éarn'st a day?

Taw. Little, God knows.
Though I be stirring earlier than the lark,
And at my labour later than the lamb,
Towards my wife and children's maintenance
I scarcely earn me three pence by the day.

Hob. Alas, the while, poor soul! I pity them;
And in thy words, as in a looking-glass,
I see the toil and travail of the country,
And quiet gain of cities' blessedness.
Heaven's will for all, and should we not respect it,
We were unworthy life.   But, bones a me,
Dost thou think to pay me twenty pound
And keep thy charge, earning a groat a day?

Taw. God bless my labours, I hope I shall.
I have this quarter, by exceeding thrift,
Bare clothing, and spare diet, scrap'd together
Five shillings in a purse, which I lay up
Towards your worship's debt.

Hob. Give it me; somewhat hath some savour.—
And yet shall I spend that which the poor labourer
    got?
No, God forbid: old Hobson ne'er will eat,
Rather than surfeit upon poor men's sweat.

Take it again, and buy thy children bread.
But soft, the mist doth break : what town is this ?

 Taw. Deptford, and it like your worship.

Enter TIMOTHY.

 Hob. Bones a me, to Deptford came I to do charity ?
I see 'twas God's appointment.—
But who comes here ? Bones a me, honest Tim !—
'Twas said in London you were bound for France,
And I determin'd to have writ by you.

 Tim. By yea and nay, Master Hobson, 'tis no untruth.
I was bound for France, landed in France, despatch'd
some secret business for a sister in France, and from her
have French tokens to deliver to the sisterhood whom
I shall first encounter in England.

 Hob. Bones a me, Tim, so speedy in your journey !
It seems your business was of much import.

 Tim. Verily it was, and it stood chiefly between two
women; and, as you know, women love to have their
business despatched.

 Hob. Mother a me, Tim, I am glad of it.
But how does my factor, John Gresham, in France?

 Tim. You gravely may better consider of that than I
can discourse; but withal, I pray you, think he is a wild
youth. There are taverns in France, yet I do not think
John Gresham is given to frequent them; and yet I
must remember you he is a youth, and youth may be
drawn to expenses. England's on this side, France on
that; the sea betwixt him and his master; but I do not
think him guilty, yet I could say.

 Hob. Mother a me, leave off these parables,
And tell me plainly, is he not a wencher?

 Tim. By yea and by nay, sir, without parable, I am
no tell-tale. I have seen him in company with Madonna
such a one, or such a one: it becomes not flesh and

blood to reveal. Your worship knows he is in France,
the sea betwixt him and you, and what a young youth
in that case is prone unto—your gravity is wise. I'll
not say so much as I saw him drinking with a French
lady or lass in a tavern, because your gravity is wise;
but if I had, it had been less than, perhaps, you imagine
on such a wild youth as he, no question, does deserve.

Hob. Mother a me, 'tis so.   In a French tavern,
Kissing the lady, and the sea betwixt us.
I am for you, Master John; thus in my gown and slip-
      pers,
And nightcap and gown, I'll step over to France.—
Here, Tawney-coat, receive thou my seal ring:
Bear it to my factor; bid him by that token
Sort thee out forty pounds' worth of such wares
As thou shalt think most beneficial.
Thou art a free man; up with thy trade again:
I'll raise thee, Goodfellow, if God say, Amen.

Taw. I know not how.

Hob. Tut, bones a me, man, peace!
Hobson will do't: thou owest me but twenty pound,
I'll venture forty more.   Timothy here shall be
Thy witness to my factor in this business.
To all our friends in London say I am gone
Over to France.—I am for you, Master John.

                              [*Exeunt.*

Enter JOHN *and Courtesan.*

Cour. Sweet youth, thou art too young, and yet scarce
      ripe
To taste the sweetness of my mellowed love.

John. That's the reason I set thy teeth on edge thus;
but thou know'st I promis'd to have a bout with thee
at our last parley, and I have come to perform my
word: name the weapon.

Cour. Nothing but kisses and enticing looks.

John. Then ward your lips well, or you'll ha' the first veney.

Cour. I have no ward but this: my tender sex
Have not the manly skill to break a thrust.
Oh, how I dote on thee! I have tried, ere now,
The sweaty Spaniard and the carousing Dane,
The foggy Dutchman, and the fiery French,
The brisk Italian, and indeed what not;
And yet of all and all, the Englishman
Shall go for me: ay, y'are the truest lovers,
The ablest last night, and the truest men
That breathe beneath the sun.

John. Why, then, the Englishman for thy money: well, my little rogue, there's no love lost, I'll assure thee. I am my master's factor, and thou hast a commodity that I must needs take up, and not enter't into his cash-book neither. Little thinks my master in England what ware I deal withal here in France; but since 'tis offer'd me at the best hand, I'll venture on't, though I be a loser by the bargain.

Cour. I would be private, lest the tell-tale air
Whisper our love. I prithee, let us in
To the inner chamber; I am jealous
Of all eyes but mine own to look upon thee:
I would have none to see thee but myself.
In amorous arms to fold thee, but myself,
To associate, talk, discourse, or dally with thee,
Clip, grasp hands, or kiss thee, but myself.

John. Who would not be a merchant venturer, and lay out for such a fair return? I shall venture the doubling of my years presently. I think I have met with a better commodity than matches, and my master cannot say but he hath met with his match. This 'tis to have the land and the sea betwixt me and my master: here can I keep my French revels, and none say so

much as black is mine eye.—Prithee, little pinkany,
bestow this jewel o' me.

Cour. This jewel's a love: ask my life, 'tis thine;
But this, an English factor, whom you know,
Gave me at his departure out of Rouen,
And I have vow'd to keep it for his sake.
Any thing but this jewel.

John. But if I could get this jewel cleanly, and
carry it him over at my return for a token, 'twere a
jest worth laughing at.—But, an thou wilt not give me
this jewel, prithee give me this same chain to wear for
thy sake.

Cour. This was another countryman's of yours:
He made me swear to keep't till his return.
Ask me aught else, 'tis thine.

John. Why, then, this ring.

Cour. That you, of all the favours that I wear,
Could find out nothing but this ring! this ring,
A toy not worth the giving; yet I sooner
Would part with life than this. A dying friend
Bequeath'd it at his death. But, honey love,
What shouldst thou talk of giving? 'tis a word
Worn out of use; it sounds not well in French:
A man should still say take, take, to his wench.

John. Then, I say take: take this, and this; still
take heed of me, lest I show you a slippery trick for
this. 'Tis the kindest wench in Christendom, but she'll
part with nothing.—Shall we have another wooing
room?

Cour. What room thou pleasest, dear heart, I
      agree:
Where'er I go, there shall be room for thee.

John. Any? then I may chance to make you wish
rather my room than my company, an you look not the
better to't.   [*They withdraw.*

Enter, at the other end of the stage, HOBSON *in his gown
and slippers.*

Hob. I have slipp'd o'er into France; and in my
    slippers,
Given all my friends the slip, to see this gallant,
My man, he that hath match'd me.   Bones a me,
The knave's a prophet, else it could not be.
He's not at his lodging, yet by an English factor,
A fellow knows not me, I was directed
Unto this house.   I'll know what business
The knave hath here.   [*Pulsat.*

Intrat Puella.

Wench. Who's there? who's at the door?

Hob. Damsel, good day: is there not a fellow here,
an Englishman?

Wench. Here's an Englishman, but none of your
fellow, neither.   I hope, sir, we are not all fellows at
foot-ball.

Hob. Nay, bones a me, girl, there's no reason we
should be fellows.   But prithee, my wench, is there not
one Jack Gresham here?

Wench. No, goodman look like a goose; but there's
one Master John Gresham, an English gentleman,
here.   And you know no manners, you should be taught
some.

Hob. Bones a me, goodman master, master ser-
    vant!
Old goodman Hobson keeps gentlemen to his men.
Jack turn'd to Master John; marry, sir reverence!
The French maid taught me manners.   Well, I hope
We shall have a sight of the gentleman.

Wench. As you use yourself, you may, and you may
not.   [*Exeunt ambo.*

Enter JOHN GRESHAM, *and Courtesan.*

John. Thou seest this jewel well becomes mine ear,
This ring my finger, and this chain mine arm.

Cour. I'll be thy jewel: at thy lips I'll hang,
And, as this ring thy finger compasseth,
So shall these arms thy waist.   These are but toys;
Let me displace them.

Intrat Puella.

Wench. Mr. John, here's a fellow below would speak
with you.

John. With me! what is he?

Wench. A simple coxcomb; I'll call him up to you.

John. Do, my sweet Buffamache.   Some carrier, or
base knave, that hangs of my liberality.—I hope 'tis not
pure Tim, come for the second part of my benevolence.
Admit him in, that he may praise our fate,
And see us in our choicest pomp and state.

Wench. Here's the fellow I told you of, sir.

Intrat HOBSON.

John. Zounds! my master.

Hob. Sancte amen!   Man John, a wenchart knave,
rack and manger knave?   Bones a me, cannot a snatch
and away serve your turn, but you must lie at rack
and manger?   Is this the ware you deal with, servant
John?

John. Chapman's ware, sir.

Hob. Sirrah, sirrah, the dealing with such ware
belongs not to our trade.   Bones a me, knave, a
'prentice must not occupy for himself, but for his master,
to any purpose.

John. And he cannot occupy for his master without
the consent of his mistress.

K

Hob. Come, y'are a knave.

John. Of your own bringing up, sir.

Hob. Besides, thou canst not keep open shop here, because thou art a foreigner, by the laws of the realm.

John. Not within the liberty ; but I hope the suburbs tolerate - any man or woman to occupy for themselves : they may do't in the city, too, an they be naturalized once.

Hob. Ay, but sirrah, I'll have none of my English 'prentices Frenchified. Bones a me, knave, I'll have thee deal with no such broken commodities.

John. Your worship must have such as the country yields, or none at all. But, I pray ye, sir, what's our trade ?

Hob. What say'st thou, knave ?

John. That your worship is a haberdasher of all wares.

Hob. Bones a me ! a haberdasher of small wares.

John. And that the worst trade in all Christendom, and especially for French women : if they know a man to be a haberdasher of small ware, they'll have no dealing with him ; and therefore, an you will have any good commodities here, you must change your copy. You never were a traveller, and therefore you know not what belongs to't. But you do clean mistake this gentlewoman, an you take her for a light wench : weigh her in equal balance, and you shall find her no such woman, no such woman, I'll assure you.

Hob. No ! what is she, then, John ?

John. Fore God, sir, I would not have you wrong the gentlewoman's repute for a world. This matressa deals for herself, and hath many sorts of ware at command : I was now bargaining with her about a certain country commodity, and, had not your coming marr'd the match, we had gone through for't. And further, should you wrong the lady's reputation here, in France,

I'll assure you they have the law of their sides. But,
to confirm your good opinion of her, this is she of whom
I took up your commodity of matches: be sorry for
your offence, and excuse you to her for shame, master.

Hob. Bones a me, knave, I cannot speak a word of
French.   •

    John. Nor she of English.   But all's one: upon her,
           master, and what
You cannot do in words, perform in dumb signs.—
What, in your slippers come to take me napping?
I'll give you what you come for instantly,
And, on the sudden, make you so aghast,
You will be glad to pardon what is past.   [*Exit.*

Hob. Madam, I cry you mercy for this wrong
Done to your ladyship: I did suspect you
For a bad liver, but I see you clear;
For which mistake I do remain your servant.

    Cour. Grand mercie, monsieur.

    Hob. How! would you my gray mare see?
An't like your ladyship, I came by water,
And neither of mare's back, nor horse back.

    Cour. No, no point parler Français?

    Hob. No, indeed, lady, my name is not Francis; your
servant, and John Hobson.

    Cour. No point.

    Hob. No points? yes, indeed, lady; I have points
at my hose, though I go untruss'd.

    Cour. No point parler.

    Hob. I have no points in my parlour, indeed; but I
have an hundred pounds' worth in my shop.

    Intrat JOHN *cum aliis Factoribus.*

    John. Tush! fear not, lads; for he knows none of you.
Do but buff out a little broken French,
And he'll never take you to be Englishmen.

                         K 2

Omn. Fact. We'll second the t'others, but manage it.

John. Be patient, I beseech you, gentlemen.

Though you be officers, appointed here

To search suspected places, as this is

A most notorious filthy bawdy-house,

And carry all old rusty fornicators,

Above the age of fifty, unto prison,

Yet know, this is an honest gentleman.

Hob. A search, and 'tis a bawdy-house ?—Why, John!

Bones a me, knave, how comes this to pass ?

1 Fact. Measar mon a moy.

Hob. How! must you have money of me? I'll know

wherefore first, by your leaves.

John. Nay, master, I would it were but a money

matter;

A cage or whipping post or so: 'tis worse.

What! an old man to chide his 'prentice hence,

As if he had some private business,

And then himself get close unto his wench!

Nay, whipping's all too good.   Had you found me so,

There had been work enough; there had been news

For England, and a whole twelve months' chiding

Of my good uncle.

2 Fact. Je vou stre sau amilt.

Hob. How ! must I go to prison for doing amiss ?

John. To prison! nay to whipping, I am sorry ;

And, to my power, I will entreat for you.

Fie, master, fie!

Hob. Bones a me, John, is not this a lady ?

John. No, by my troth, master; such as in the

garden-alleys.

Joan's as good as this French lady.

Hob. Is not this gentlewoman a dealer,

And hath she not a good commodity ?

John. Yes, by my faith, sir, I confess both.

Hob. Hath she not ware?

John. She hath, and at a reasonable reckoning.

Hob. And may not, then, a chapman deal with her?

John. Marry may ye, sir; and I'll send news to your
  wife of your dealing.

The cause of your coming to France shall be known,

And what second hand commodities you took up

Since your coming: my mistress in England shall know

What utterance you have for your small wares in France.

Pen and ink!—I'll set it down in black and white.

 Hob. Bones a me, John! what, John! why, honest
  John!

 John. "Hearty commendations—understand—reverend Master Hobson found with a whore in Rouen—
place, a common bawdy-house—must be whipped."

 Hob. No more, good John!

 John. You have had none yet—" whipp'd about the
  town."

 Hob. Sweet, honest John! why, bones a me, knave
  John!

 John. "In witness whereof, all these honest gentlemen, eye-witnesses, have set to their hands."—Nay, my
mistress shall know't, that's flat. Are there not wenches
enow in England, but you must walk over sea in your
slippers, and venture (being not shod) to come into
France, a wenching? what, an old man, too? She shall
know what a slippery trick you would have served her
in your slippers in France.

 Hob. Nay, bones a me, John; friends, sweet John,
  all friends;

I do confess th'ast overreach'd thy master.

Ca me, ca thee: conceal this from my wife,

And I'll keep all thy knavery from thine uncle.

 John. Well sir, in hope of amendment, I am content,
  and yet ——

Hob. Nay, bones a me, I'll take you at your word.
Besides, I hope these honest gentlemen
Will save my credit.

John. I'll entreat for you.

Hob. 'Tis logic to me, sir; I understand you not.

John. Marry, sir, they say if you will walk with them
to their lodgings, for my sake they invite you to dinner.

Hob. God a mercy, gentlemen; God a mercy, John.
But, bones a me, where are their lodgings?

John. Hard by; for why do you ask?

Hob. I hope they'll bring me to no more bawdy-
houses;
I would not be taken napping again for two and one.
But, gentlemen, I'll accept of courtesy, and then, John,
You shall with me to England: we'll show France
Our backs.   An you will needs deal for yourself
Afore your time, you shall do't in England.—
Will you walk, gentlemen?

Cour. Adieu, monsieur: and, Gresham, farewell too.
No more of French love, no more French loss shall do.

[*Exeunt.*

Enter Sir THOMAS RAMSEY, *being Mayor, Sheriff,
Sword-bearer, &c.*

Sir Thos. Well said, my masters.   See all things be
ready
To give her Majesty such entertain
As may grace London, and become the state
Her highness brings along.   Where's the Queen now?

Sword. She comes along the Strand from Somerset
House,
Through Temple Bar, down Fleet Street and the Cheap,
The north side of the Burse to Bishopsgate,
And dines at Master Gresham's; and appoints
To return on the south side, through Cornhill:

And there, when she hath view'd the rooms above
And walks below, she'll give name to the Burse.

Sher. The streets are fit, and all the companies
Plac'd in their liveries 'gainst her return.
But, my Lord Mayor, shall these Ambassadors
This day have audience?

Sir Thos. Admittance, if not audience, was granted:
See, therefore, trumpets and all kinds of music
Be plac'd against her royal interview.
The steps with arras spread where she ascends;
Besides, give charge unto the shopkeepers
To make their best shows in the upper rooms,
Because the Queen intends to compass it.

Sher. 'Tis done, my lord.   [*Trumpets afar off.*
Sir Thos. The Queen hath din'd: the trumpets sound
    already,
And give note of her coming.—Bid the waits
And hautboys to be ready at an instant.

Enter, at one door, the Queen, LEICESTER, SUSSEX, *Lords,*
    GRESHAM: *at the other,* CASSIMIR, *the French and
    Florentine Ambassadors, Sir* THOMAS RAMSEY, &c.

Queen. Leicester and Sussex, are those the Ambas-
    sadors?

Leic. They are, dread sovereign: he that foremost
    stands,
The Emperor's; the second is the French;
The last is the Florentine.

Queen. We will receive them.
        [*Here the Queen entertains the Ambassadors, and
            in their several languages confers with them.*
Sussex and Leicester, place the Ambassadors.
We at our Court of Greenwich will dilate
Further of these designs.   Where's Gresham?

Gresh. Your humble subject and servant.

Queen. Our leisure now serves to survey your Burse.
A goodly frame, a rare proportion!
This city, our great chamber, cannot show us,
To add unto our fame, a monument
Of greater beauty.—Leicester, what say'st thou?

Leic. That I, my sovereign, have not seen the like.

Queen. Sussex, nor you?

Suss. Madam, not I.   This Gresham's work of stone
Will live to him, when I am dead and gone.

Enter HOBSON.

Hob. God bless thy grace, Queen Bess!

Queen. Friend, what are you?

Hob. Knowest thou not me, Queen? then, thou
        knowest nobody.
Bones a me, Queen, I am Hobson; old Hobson,
By the stocks: I am sure you know me.

Queen. What is he, Leicester? dost thou know this
        fellow?—
Gresham, or you?

Gresh. May it please your Majesty,
He is a rich, substantial citizen.

Hob. Bones a me, woman, send to borrow money
Of one you do not know! there's a new trick.
Your grace sent to me by a pursuivant,
And by a privy seal, to lend your highness
An hundred pound: I, hearing that my Queen
Had need of money, and thinking you had known me,
Would needs upon the bearer force two hundred.
The Queen should have had three, rather than fail;
Ay, by this hand.   Queen Bess, I am old Hobson,
A haberdasher, and dwelling by the stocks.
When thou seest money with thy grace is scant,
For twice five hundred pound thou shalt not want.

Queen. Upon my bond?

Hob. No, no, my sovereign;
I'll take thine own word, without scrip or scroll.

Queen. Thanks, honest Hobson: as I am true maid,
I'll see myself the money back repaid.
Thou without grudging lend'st, thy purse is free;
Honest as plain.

Suss. A true, well meaning man, I warrant him.

Gresh. Your Majesty promised to give the name
To my new Burse.

Queen. Gresham, we will.—A herald, and a trumpet!

Leic. A herald, and a trumpet!

Queen. Proclaim through every high street of this city,
This place to be no longer call'd a Burse,
But, since the building's stately, fair, and strange,
Be it for ever call'd the Royal Exchange.

        [A flourish here.
And whilst this voice flies through the streets forth-
  right,
Arise, Sir Thomas Gresham, now a knight.—
Be our Ambassadors conducted all
Unto their several lodgings.—This twenty-third of
  January,
A thousand, five hundred, and seventy, Elizabeth
Christens this famous work.   Now, to our Court
Of Greenwich.—Gresham, thanks for our good cheer.
We to our people, they to us are dear. *[Exeunt.*

  Enter Dr. NOWELL *and Lady* RAMSEY.

Lady R. What think you of my husband, Master
  Dean?

Dr. Now. As of all men: we are mortal, made of clay,
Now healthful, now crazy, now sick, now well,
Now live, now dead; and then to heaven or hell.

Lady R. It cheers my heart, now, in his deep of
  sickness,

He is so charitable, and so well addicted
Unto the poor's relief.

 Dr. Now. It joys me, too.
Great is the number of the rich in show
About the city, but of the charitable
There are but few.

 Lady R. Amongst these, I hold Hobson well de-
  serves
To be rank'd equal with the bountiful'st.
He hath rais'd many falling, but especially
One Master Goodfellow, once call'd Tawney-coat,
But now an able citizen, late chosen
A master of the Hospital.

 Dr. Now. I know him well;
A good, sufficient man; and since he purchas'd
His freedom in the city, Heaven hath bless'd
His travail with increase.

 Lady R. I have known old Hobson
Sit with his neighbour Gunter, a good man,
In Christ's Church, morn by morn, to watch poor
  couples
That come there to be married, and to be
Their common fathers, and give them in the church,
And some few angels for a dower to boot.
Besides, they two are call'd the common gossips,
To witness at the font for poor men's children.
None they refuse that on their help do call;
And, to speak truth, they're bountiful to all.

Enter HOBSON.

 Hob. Good morrow, Master Doctor, my good lady.
Bones a me, woman, thou look'st sad to-day:
Thou hast not drunk a cup of sack this morning.

 Lady R. We have been dealing of our charity
This morning to poor soldiers, such as want.

Hob. Heaven's blessing of your heart: need must be
    fed.

Let us, that have it, give the hungry bread.

Enter GOODFELLOW, *alias Tawney-coat.*

Taw. Where's Master Hobson?

Hob. My new elected master of the Hospital,
What hasty news with you?

Taw. Oh, sir, the love I bear you makes me chary
Of your good name; your credit's dear to me.
You never were condemn'd for any thing,
Since I had first acquaintance with your name,
As now you are.   You have done a deed this day,
That hath from you ta'en all good thoughts away.

Hob. Where? bones a me!   Why? speak, why?

Taw. This day you have pursued the law severely
Against one Timothy, that stole from you
A hundred pound; and he's condemn'd for it,
And this day he must die.

Hob. Bones, man! 'tis not so?

Taw. He is by this half way to Tyburn gone.
The suit was follow'd in John Gresham's name;
How can you, then, avow you know it not?

Hob. A horse! a horse! cart horse, malt horse, any
    thing,
To save the knave's life!—I protest, I swear,
This was the first time that I heard the knave
Hath been in any trouble.   Bones a me,
'Twas done without my knowledge.

Taw. Young Gresham in his name pursued his
    life.

Hob. They are knaves both.—A horse!
A hundred thousand pound cannot make a man;
A hundred shall not hang one by my means:
Men are more worth than money, Mr. Goodfellow.

Come, help me to a horse.   The next I meet,
To save the knave's life, gallops through the street.
> [*Exeunt* HOBSON *and Tawney-coat.*

Dr. Now. Men are more worth than money—a' says
  true;
'Tis said by many, but maintain'd by few.
  Lady R. He is plain and honest: how many great
    professors
Live in this populous city, that make show
Of greater zeal, yet will not pay so dear
For a transgressor's life.   But few are found
To save a man would lose a hundred pound.

Enter Tawney-coat.

  Dr. Now. So suddenly return'd?
  Taw. He rid too fast for me.   He hath been at
    buffets
With a poor collier, and upon his horse
Is, without saddle, bridle, boots, or spurs,
Gallop'd towards St. Giles.
  Dr. Now. They will take him for a madman.
  Taw. All's one to him: he does not stand on bravery,
So he may do men good.   Good deeds excel;
And, though but homely done, may be done well.
  Lady R. Heaven prosper his intent—Now, Master
    Doctor,
And Master Goodfellow, let me crave your companies
To see my crazy husband, who hath made you
One of his executors, and would use your pains
In these extremes of sickness.
  Dr. Now. I am pleas'd;
I'll give him physic for a soul diseas'd.   [*Exeunt.*

Enter three Lords.

  1st Lord. You are an early riser, my good lord.

2nd Lord. The blood of youth that traffics in the
Court
Must not be sluggish; your kind remembrance.

3rd Lord. My very good lord, we, that are stars
that wait
Upon the train of such a Cynthia
Under which we live, must not be tardy.

1st Lord. You have said true: we are starters in one
hour,
And our attendance is to wait on such a Queen,
Whose virtue all the world——But to leave that,
Which every tongue is glad to commune with,
Since Monsieur's first arrival in the land,
The time that he was here, and the time since,
What royalty hath been in England's Court,
Both princely revelling and warlike sport!

2nd Lord. Such sports do fitly fit our nation,
That foreign eyes beholding what we are,
May rather seek our peace than wish our war.

3rd Lord. Heaven bless our sovereign from her foes'
intent!
The peace we have is by her government.

Enter Dr. PARRY.

1st Lord. Master Doctor Parry.

2nd Lord. Good morrow, Master Doctor.

3rd Lord. You are an early riser, sir.

Dr. Par. My lord, my lord, my very good lord.

1st Lord. This summer morning makes us covetous
To take the profit of the pleasant air.

Dr. Par. 'Tis healthful to be stirring in a morning.

2nd Lord. It hath pleas'd the Queen to show him
many favours.

3rd Lord. You say but right; and since his last disgrace,

The cause so great it had surely touch'd his life,
Had not the Queen been gracious, he seems at
  Court
A man more gracious in our sovereign's eye,
Than greater subjects.

    2nd Lord. She hath given him much preferment,
In greatest place grac'd him with conference,
Ask'd for him in his absence; and, indeed,
Made known to us he is one in her regard.

    3rd Lord. But did you never hear the cause of his
  disgrace?

    2nd Lord. He did intend the murder of a gentleman,
One Mr. Hare, here, of the Inner Temple,
And so far brought his purpose to effect,
That Mr. Hare being private in his chamber,
He watching, as he thought, fit time, broke in upon
  him;
But he, assaulted, so behav'd himself,
That he did guard himself, and attach'd him.
From whence he was committed unto Newgate,
And at the Sessions, by twelve honest men
Found guilty of burglary, and condemn'd to die;
And had died, had her grace not pardon'd him.

    3rd Lord. She is a gracious princess unto all.
Many she raiseth, wisheth none should fall.

    1st Lord. Fie, Master Doctor!
Your face bears not the habit it was wont,
And your discourse is alter'd: what's the matter?

    Dr. Par. And if my brow be sad, or my face pale,
They do belie my heart, for I am merry.

    1st Lord. Men being, as you are, so great in grace
With such a royal princess, have no reason.

            Enter a Gentleman.

    Gent. Room, gentlemen, for my Lord High Steward!

Enter the Earl of Leicester; and all the Lords flock after
*   him, and Exeunt.   Manet Dr.* PARRY.

Dr. Par. The discontent desire to be alone:
My wishes are made up, for they are gone.
Here are no blabs but this, and this one clock
I'll keep from going with a double lock.
Yet it will strike: this day it must be done.
What must be done, what must this engine do?
A deed of treason hath prepar'd me to.
These two, these two; why, they had life by
        her,
And shall these two kill their deliverer,
The life that makes me rise? these once my sin
Had forfeited; her mercy pardon'd me.
I had been eaten up with worms, ere this,
Had not her mercy given a life to this;
And yet these hands, if I perform my oath,
Must kill that life that gave a life to both.
I have ta'en the Sacrament to do't, conferr'd
With Cardinal Como about it, and receiv'd
Full absolution from his holiness;
Been satisfied by many holy fathers,
During my travels both in France and Italy,
The deed is just and meritorious.
And yet I am troubled, when I do remember
The excellency of her Majesty;
And I would fain desist, but that I know
How many vows of mine are gone to Heaven,
My letters, and my promises on earth,
To holy fathers and grave Catholics,
That I would do't for good of Catholics,
Then, in the garden where this day she walks.
Her graces I will cast behind mine eyes,
And by a subject's hand a sovereign dies.

Enter Gentleman.

Gent. Clear the way, gentlemen, for the Queen!
Master Doctor Parry.   [*Exit Gentleman.*
  Dr. Par. Oh, let me see a difference in this man.
Before this Queen (that I am come to kill)
Show'd [me] the gracious eye of her respect,
And gave me countenance 'mongst greatest earls,
This man was forwarder to thrust me forth,
Than now he is humble to accept me in.
If, then, her grace hath honour'd me so much,
How can this hand give her a treacherous touch?
The trumpets speak; Heaven! what shall I do?
Even what hell and my damn'd heart shall thrust me to.

Enter Queen, LEICESTER, *and Lords.*

  Queen. Fair day, my lords.   You are all larks, this
        morning;
Up with the sun: you are stirring early.
  Leic. We are all subject to your sovereign light.
  Queen. That you call duty, we accept as love,
And we do thank you; nay, we thank you all:
'Tis not to one, but 'tis in general.
  Leic. The Queen would walk apart: forbear, my
        lords.   [*They retire.*
  Dr. Par. Now, what makes me shake?
Do angels guard her, or doth Heaven partake
Her refuge?
  Queen. In such a garden may a sovereign
Be taught her loving subjects to maintain.
Each plant, unto his nature and his worth
Having full cherishing, it springeth forth.
Weeds must be weeded out, yet weeded so,
Till they do hurt, let them in Heaven's name grow.
  Dr. Par. Now, Queen!   [*He offers to shoot.*

Queen. Who's there? my kind friend, Master Doctor
    Parry?

Dr. Par. My most dread sovereign.

Queen. Why do you tremble, Master Doctor? Have
    you any suit to us?

Shake not at us; we do our subjects love.

Or does thy face show signs of discontent

Through any heavy want oppresseth thee?

Though at our Court of Greenwich thou wert cross'd,

In sueing to be Master of St. Katharine's,

To do thee good, seek out a better place:

She'll give thee that, the which hath given thee grace.

Dr. Par. I know your love, dread Queen.—Now!

Queen. Master Doctor, about the talk we had to-
    gether

Of English fugitives that seek my life:

You told me of them; I am beholding to you.

Dr. Par. I did no more than duty.—O, happy time!

Queen. And will they still persist? do they desire my
    blood,

That wake, when I should sleep, to do them good?

Dr. Par. Madam!

Queen. Oh, my Maker!—Parry! villain! traitor!

What doest thou with that dag?

Dr. Par. Pardon, dread sovereign.

Queen. Pardon, thou villain, shows thou art a traitor.

Treason, my lords! treason!

Enter the Lords.

Leic. Ha! by the bless'd place of Heaven, treason,
    and we so near?

A traitor with a dag! God's holy mother!—

Lords, guard the Queen.—Are you not frighten'd,
    madam?

I'll play the sergeant to arrest the wretch.

Queen. Be not so rash, good Leicester: he's dead
    already;
Struck with remorse of that he was to do.
Pray, let me speak with him.—Say, Master Doctor,
Wherein I have deserv'd an ill of you,
Unless it were an ill in pardoning you?
What have I done toward you, to seek my life,
Unless it were in taking you to grace?
    Dr. Par. Mercy, dread Queen!
    Queen. I thank my God I have mercy to remit
A greater sin, if you repent for it.   Arise.
    Leic. My lords, what do you mean? take hence that
    villain.
Let her alone, she'll pardon him again.—
Good Queen, we know you are too merciful
To deal with traitors of this monstrous kind.—
Away with him to the Tower, then to death.—
A traitor's death shall such a traitor have,
That seeks his sovereign's life that did him save.
    Queen. Good Leicester!
    Leic. Good Queen, you must be rul'd.   [*Exeunt.*

Enter JOHN GRESHAM.

John. Nay, 'sfoot, Jack, hold on thy resolution. They
say, that may happen in one hour that happens not
again in seven year: an I should chance to take her in
the right vein, and she kindly bestow herself upon me,
why, then, there's a man made from nothing; for, before God, I have spent all, and am not worth anything.
And, indeed, unless this same good old Lady Ramsey
take some pity upon me, and take me for better for
worse, God knows in which of the two Compters I shall
keep my next Christmas in! But, by this hand, if she
will accept of me in this miserable estate that I am in
now—for, before God, I have neither money nor credit,

as I am an honest man—and that's more, I am afraid,
than any man will believe of me—I'll forswear all
women but her, and will not kiss any of my neighbours'
wives for a kingdom.—Here's the house: I'll knock at
the door.—What, shall I do't in the cavalier humour,
with, "Who's within, there? ho!" or in the Puritan
humour, with, "By your leave, good brother?" Faith,
in neither; for in the one I shall be taken for a swag-
gering knave, and in the other, to be an hypocritical
fool; but, honest Jack, in thine own honest humour.
Plain dealing's a jewel, and I have used it so long, I am
next door to a beggar.

Enter two Creditors.

But, God's precious! what a plague make these here?
These two are two of my creditors: I must stop their
mouths, fleet them from hence, or all the fat's in the fire.

1st. Master Gresham, you are well met.

John. I hope, gentlemen, you will say so anon. But
you are alone, are you not?

2nd. Master Gresham, why do you ask?

John. A man hath reason to ask, being as I am, that
never seeth his creditors but is afeard of the catchpole.
But you are kind, my friends; and, I thank you, you
will bear with me.

1st. Ay, but, Master Gresham, a man may bear till
his back break.

John. Ay, porters may; but you that are substantial,
honest citizens, there is no fear to be made of your
breaking. You know there's no man so low, but God
can raise him; and though I am now out at heels, or so,
as you think, I am in the way of preferment, and hope
to be able to pay every man within this hour.

1st. We should be glad to see it.

2nd. But how, pray, sir?

John. How? why, very easily, if I can compass it. The truth is, though you would little think it, I am suitor for my Lady Ramsey.

1st. But I dare swear she is no suitor to you.

Enter Lady RAMSEY *and Dr.* NOWELL.

John. Why, that's true, too; for if she were a suitor to me, we should be man and wife straight, and you should have your money within this half hour. But look; look where she comes: as you are good men, mum; patience, and pray for my proceedings. If I do speed, as I am partly persuaded, you shall have your own, with the advantage: if I should be cross'd, you know the worst; forbearance is no acquittance. But mum! if it prove a match, and any of you should chance to be in the Compter, you know, my marriage being spread, my word will be current then. Mum.

Dr. Now. Madam, you are welcome into Lombard Street.

Lady R. I thank your courtesy, good Master Dean.

John. See how fortunately all things chance. If it happen, as I hope it will, she taking a liking to me, here is a priest to marry us presently.—Madam——

Lady R. Would you any business with me, sir?

John. 'Faith, lady, necessary business; and, not to go far about the bush, I am come to be a suitor unto you. And you know the fashion of young men, when they come a wooing to ancient widows, the way to speed is to begin thus.

Lady R. You are very forward, sir.

John. You would say so, lady, if you knew how forward I would be. But, madam, you are rich, and by my troth, I am very poor, and I have been, as a man should say, stark naught; but he goes far that never turns; and if now I have a desire to mend, and being

in so good a way, you know how uncharitable it were
in you to put me out of it.   You may make an honest
man of me, if it please you; and when thou hast made
me one, by my troth, Mall, I'll keep myself, for I am a
gentleman both by the father's side and mother's side ;
and, though I have not the muck of the world, I have a
great deal of good love, and I prithee accept of it.

Lady R. Master Dean,
Do you know this gentleman's business with me?

Dr. Now. Not I, believe me, madam.

John. I shall have her sure.—Why, I'll tell you, sir.
My lady here is a comely, ancient, rich widow, and I
am an honest, proper, poor young man, remembering
still I am a gentleman: now, what good her riches may
do my poverty, your gravity may guess; save a soul,
perhaps, Master Dean.   Look you, sir: it is but giving
my hand into hers, and hers into mine.   Master Dean,
I protest before God she hath my heart already; and
with some three or four words, which I know you have
by rote, make us two, my lady and I, one, till death us
depart.

Lady R. This gentleman thinks that to be a matter
of nothing.—But do you love me as you protest?

John. Love you, madam? I love you, by this hand—
I shall have her, sure.—Friends, you see how the business
goes forward; bring me your bills to-morrow morning;
or, upon the hope that I have, you may leave them
with me: I shall be able to discharge.—Ha! ha! Jack.

Lady R. How will you maintain me, sir, if I should
marry you?

John. Maintain! what need is there ask that question?
'Fore, thou hast maintenance enough for thee and I too,
If I should marry you. Friends, you see how it goes
now: to-morrow, within an hour after I am married, I
must take the upper hand of my ... and the next

Sunday, I, that was scarce worthy to sit in the belfry,
the churchwardens fetch me, and seat me in the chancel.

Lady R. Master Dean, I protest, never since I was
     widow
Did man make so much love to me.—
Sir, for your love I am much beholding to you.

John. Do Mall, prithee do not think it so.—Be chosen
one of the Common Council, or one of the Masters of
the Hospital, so perhaps I shall never become it. Marry,
if I should be chosen one of the Masters of Bridewell
for some of my old acquaintance, 'foot, I would take it
upon me: vice must be corrected, vice must be corrected.

Lady R. Fill me a large cup full of hippocras,
And bring me hither twenty pound in gold.

John. And one of your husband's livery gowns. So,
now you trouble yourself too much: that gold is to
contract us withal.—A simple morning; friends, you
cannot beat me down with your bills.—Master Dean of
Paul's, I pray you stay and dine with me; you shall not
say me nay: the oftener you come the more welcome.

Dr. Now. You are merry, sir.

John. I thank God, and all the world may see, I have
     no other cause,
That I am likely to be so well bestowed.

Lady R. Sir, you shall not say the love you show'd
     to me
Was entertain'd but with kind courtesy:
This for your love unto your health I drink.
Pledge me.

John. Ay, by my troth, Mall, will I, were it as deep
as a well.

Lady R. Now, for your pains, there is twenty pound
     in gold.
Nay, take the cup, too, sir. Thanks for your love;
And were my thoughts bent unto marriage,

I rather would with you, that seem thus wild,
Than one that hath worse thoughts, and seems mo mild.

John. 'Foot, will you not have me, then?

Lady R. Yes, when I mean to marry any one;
And that not whilst I live.

John. See how a man may be deceived! I thought
I should have been sure, by this time.—Well, though I
shall not have you, I shall have this with a good will.

Lady R. With all my heart; and for the love you
        have shown,
Wish it to thrive with you, even as mine own.

1st. To-morrow shall we attend your worship?

2nd. Sir, here's my bill; it comes to twenty pound.

John. Friends, Plowden's proverb, " the case is
altered:" and, by my troth, I have learn'd you a lesson;
forbearance is no acquittance.

Lady R. What men are these?

John. 'Faith, madam, men that have my hand, though
not for my honesty, yet for the money that I owe them.

Lady R. What doth he owe you?

1st. Fifty pound, madam.

Lady R. What you?

2nd. A hundred marks.

Lady R. I'll pay you both.—And, sir, to do you good,
To all your creditors I'll do the like.

John. That's said like a kind wench;
And, though we never meet again,
We will have one buss more at parting.—
And now, faith, I have all my wild oats sown,
And if I can grow rich by the help of this,
I'll say I rose by Lady Ramsey's kiss.   [*Exeunt.*

Enter Chorus.

From fifty-eight, the first year of her reign,
We come to eighty-eight, and of her reign

The thirtieth year.   This Queen inaugurated,
And strongly planted in her people's heart,
Was in her youth solicited in marriage
By many princely heirs of Christendom,
Especially by Philip, King of Spain,
Her sister's husband ; who, to achieve his ends,
Had got a dispensation from the Pope :
But, after many treats and embassies,
Finding his hopes in her quite frustrated,
Aims all his stratagems, plots, and designs,
Both to the utter ruin of our land,
And our religion.   But th' undaunted Queen,
Fearing no threats, but willing to strike first,
Sets forth a fleet of one-and-twenty sail
To the West Indies, under the conduct
Of Francis Drake and Christopher Carlisle ;
Who set on Cape de Verd, then Hispaniola,
Setting on fire the towns of St. Anthony
And St. Dominique.   The proud Spaniard,
Enraged at this affront, sends forth a fleet,
Three whole years in preparing, to subvert,
Ruin, and quite depopulate this land.
Imagine you now see them under sail,
Swell'd up with many a proud, vainglorious boast,
And newly enter'd in our English coast.   [*Exit.*

Enter the Duke of Medina, Don PEDRO, JOHN MARTINUS,
RICALDUS, *and other Spaniards.*

   Med. We are where we long wish'd to be at last ;
And now this elephant's burden, our Armada,
Three years an embryon, is at length produc'd,
And brought into the world to live at sea.
Non sufficit orbis, our proud Spanish motto
By th' English mock'd, and found at Carthagena,
Shall it not now take force ?

Can England satisfy our avarice,
That worlds cannot suffice ?   What thinks Don Pedro?

  Ped. Alphonsus Perez Gusman,
Duke of Medina and Sidonia,
And royal general of our great Armada,
I think we come too strong.   What's our design
Against a petty island govern'd by a woman?
I think, instead of military men,
Garnish'd with arms and martial discipline,
She, with a feminine train
Of her bright ladies, beautifull'st and best,
Will meet us in their smocks, willing to pay
Their maidenheads for ransom.   ·

  Med. Think'st thou so, Don Pedro?

  Ped. I therein am confident;
And partly that our King of Spain
Hath been at charge of such a magazine,
When half our men and ammunition
Might have been spar'd.

  Med. Thou putt'st me now in mind
Of the Grand Signior, who, (some few years since)
When as the great Ambassador of Spain
Importun'd him for aid against the land
Styl'd by the title of the Maiden Isle,
Calls for a map: now, when the Ambassador   ·
Had show'd him th' Indies, all America,
Some parts of Asia, and Europa too,
Climes that took up the greatest part o' th' card,
And finding England but a spot of earth,
Or a few acres, if at all, compar'd
To our so large and spacious provinces,
Denies him aid, as much against his honour
To fight with such a centuple of odds;
But gave him this advice: " Were I," said he,
" As your great King of Spain, out of my kingdoms

I'd press or hire so many pioneers,
As with their spades and mattocks should dig up
This wart of earth, and cast it in the sea."
And well methought he spake.

   Ped. We have shown ourselves,
But are as yet unfought with.

   Med. All their hearts
Are dead within 'em; we, I fear, shall find
Their seas unguarded, and their shores unmann'd,
And conquer without battle.

   Rical. All their honours
And offices we have dispos'd already.
There's not a noble family in Spain,
In Naples, Portugal, nay, Italy,
That hath not in our fleet some eminent person
To share in this rich booty.

   Med. John Martinus Ricaldus, you, our prime navi-
      gator,
Since fam'd Columbus or great Magelhaens,
Give us a brief relation of the strength
And potency of this our great Armada,
Christen'd, by th' Pope, the Navy Invincible.

   Rical. Twelve mighty galleons of Portingal;
Fourteen great ships of Biscay, of Castile;
Eleven tall ships of Andalusia;
Sixteen galleons, fourteen of Guipuscoa;
Ten sail that run by th' name o' th' Eastern fleet;
The ships of Urcas, Zaibras, Naples; galleys,
Great galliasses, fly boats, pinnaces,
Amounting to the number of an hundred
And thirty tight, tall sail; the most of them
Seeming like castles built upon the sea.

   Med. And what can all their barges, cockboats,
      oars,
Small vessels (better to be said to creep

Than sail upon the ocean) do 'gainst these?
They are o'ercome already.

 Rical. All their burdens,
Fifty-seven thousand, eight hundred, sixty-eight, ton;
In them, nineteen thousand, two hundred, ninety-five,
  soldiers,
Two thousand, eight hundred, and eighty, galley slaves,
Eight thousand, six hundred, and fifty, mariners,
Two thousand, six hundred, and thirty, piece of ord-
  nance,
Culverin, and cannon.

 Med. Half these would suffice;
Nor have we need of such surplusage,
Against their petty fly boats.

Enter a Spaniard.

 Span. We have discover'd,
Riding along the coasts of France and Dunkirk,
An English navy.

 Med. Of what strength? what force?

 Span. Their number small, yet daring, as it seems:
Their ships are but low built, yet swift of sail.
Whether their purpose be to fight, I know not;
They bear up bravely with us.

 Ped. Cast our fleet
Into a wide and semicircled moon;
And, if we can but once encompass them,
We'll make the sea their graves, and themselves food
For the sea worm call'd haddock.

 Med. Let's sail on
Towards the Thames' mouth, and there disburden us
Of our land soldiers;
And if the Prince of Parma keep his appointment,
Who (with a thousand able men-at-arms,
Old soldiers, and of most approved discipline)

Lies garrison'd at Dunkirk, we at once
Will swallow up their nation, and our word
Be from henceforth Victoria!

   Omnes. Victoria! Victoria!   [*Exeunt.*

   Med. Had we no other forces in our fleet,
Nor men, nor arms, nor ammunition,
Powder, nor ordnance, but our empty bottoms,
Ballast with the Pope's blessing, and our navy
Christen'd by him the Navy Invincible,
We had enough: what's more's unnecessary.
Nor think we threaten England all in vain;
'Tis ours, and we here christen it New Spain.

   Omnes. Victoria! Victoria!

Drum and colours. Enter the Earl of Leicester, Sir
   ANTHONY BROWN, *the Earl of Hunsdon, bearing the*
   standard, Queen ELIZABETH, *completely armed, and*
   Soldiers.

   Queen. A stand!—From London thus far have we
      marched;
Here pitch our tents.   How do you call this place?

   Leic. The town you see, to whom these downs
      belong,
Gives them to name the plains of Tilbury.

   Queen. Be this, then, styl'd our camp at Tilbury;
And the first place we have been seen in arms,
Or thus accoutred, here we fix our foot,
Not to stir back, were we sure here t'encounter
With all the Spanish vengeance threaten'd us,
Came it in fire and thunder.   Know, my subjects,
Your Queen hath now put on a masculine spirit,
To tell the bold and daring what they are,
Or what they ought to be; and such as faint,
Teach them, by my example, fortitude.
Nor let the best prov'd soldier here disdain

A woman should conduct a host of men,
To their disgrace or want of precedent.
Have you not read of brave Zenobia,
An Eastern queen, who fac'd the Roman legions,
Even in their pride and height of potency,
And in the field encounter'd personally
Aurelianus Cæsar?   Think in me
Her spirit survives, Queen of this western isle,
To make the scorn'd name of Elizabeth
As frightful and as terrible to Spain
As was Zenobia's to the State of Rome.
Oh! I could wish them landed, and in view,
To bid them instant battle, ere march farther
Into my land.   This is my vow, my rest;
I'll pave their way with this my virgin breast.

   Leic. But, madam, ere that day come,
There will be many a bloody nose, ay, and crack'd
    crown:
We shall make work for surgeons.

   Queen. I hope so, Leicester.—For you, Sir Anthony
    Brown,
Though your religion and recusancy
Might, in these dangerous and suspicious times,
Have drawn your loyalty into suspense,
Yet have you herein amply clear'd yourself,
By bringing us five hundred men, well arm'd,
And your own self in person.

   Sir Antho. Not only those, but all that I enjoy,
Are at your highness' service.

   Queen. Now, Lord Hunsdon,
The Lord-Lieutenant of our force by land
Under our general, Leicester, what thinkest thou
Of their Armada, christen'd by the Pope
The Navy Invincible?

   Huns. That there's a power above both them and us,

That can their proud and haughty menaces
Convert to their own ruins.

   Queen. Thinkest thou so, Hunsdon?
No doubt it will.—Let me better survey my camp.
Some wine, there!—A health to all my soldiers.

                         [*Flourish of trumpets.*

Methinks I do not see, 'mongst all my troops,
One with a courtier's face, but all look soldier-like.—

                        [*A peal of shot within.*

Whence came this sound of shot?

   Leic. It seems, the navy
Styl'd by the Pope the Navy Invincible,
Riding along the coast of France and Dunkirk,
Discover'd first by Captain Thomas Fleming,
Is met and fought with by your admiral.

   Queen. Heaven prosper their defence!
Oh! had God made us man-like, like our mind,
We'd not be here fenc'd in a mure of arms,
But have been present at these sea alarms.   [*Horn.*

Enter First Post.

Make way, there!—What's the news?

   1st Post. Heaven bless your Majesty!
Your royal fleet bids battle to the Spaniard,
Whose number, with advantage of the wind,
Gains them great odds; but the undaunted worth
And well known valour of your admiral,
Sir Francis Drake, and Martin Furbisher,
John Hawkins, and your other English captains,
Takes not away all hope of victory.

   Queen. Canst thou describe the manner of the fight,
And where the royal navies first encounter'd?

   Post. From Dover cliff we might discern them join
'Twixt that and Calais; there the fight began.
Sir Francis Drake, Vice-Admiral, was first

Gave an onset to this great Armada of Spain;
The manner thus.   With twenty-five sail,
Those ships of no great burden, yet well mann'd,
For in that dreadful conflict few or none
Of your ships royal came within the sight,
This Drake, I say, (whose memory shall live
While this great world, he compass'd first, shall last)
Gave order that his squadrons, one by one,
Should follow him some distance, steers his course,
But none to shoot till he himself gave fire.
Forward he steer'd, as far before the rest
As a good musket can well bear at twice,
And, as a spy, comes to survey their fleet,
Which seem'd like a huge city built on the sea.
They shot, and shot, and emptied their broadsides
At his poor single vessel: he sails on,
Yet all this while no fire was seen from him.
The rest behind, longing for action,
Thought he had been turn'd coward, that had done
All this for their more safety.   He now finding
Most of their present fury spent at him,
Fires a whole tier at once, and having emptied
A full broadside, the rest came up to him,
And did the like, undaunted.   Scarce the last
Had pass'd by them, but Drake had clear'd the
        sea;
For, ere th' unwieldy vessels could be stirr'd,
Or their late emptied ordnance charg'd again,
He takes advantage both of wind and tide,
And the same course he took in his progress
Doth in his back return keep the same order,
Scouring along, as if he would besiege them
With a new wall of fire, in all his squadrons
Leaving no charge that was not bravely mann'd:
Insomuch, that blood as visibly was seen

To pour out of their portholes, in such manner
As, after showers i' th' city, spouts spill rain.
And thus Drake bade them welcome: what after
    happen'd,
Such a huge cloud of smoke environ'd us,
We could not well discover.

    Queen. There's for thy speed;
And England ne'er want such a Drake at need.

        Enter the Second Post.

Th' art welcome: what canst thou relate,
Touching this naval conflict?

    2nd Post. Since Drake's first onset, and our fleet
    retir'd,
The Spanish navy, being link'd and chain'd
Like a half moon or to a full bent bow,
Attend advantage; where, amongst the rest,
Sir Martin Frobisher, blinded with smoke,
By chance is fallen into the midst of them,
Still fighting 'gainst the extremity of odds,
Where he, with all his gallant followers,
Are folded in death's arms.

    Queen. If he survive, he shall be nobly ransom'd;
If he be dead,
Yet he shall live in immortality.
How fares our admiral?

    2nd Post. Bravely directs,
And with much judgment. England never bred
Men that a sea fight better managed.

    Queen. It cheers my blood; and if so Heaven be
    pleas'd,
For some neglected duty in ourself,
To punish [us] with loss of these brave spirits,
His will be done; yet will we pray for them.—
What says valiant Leicester?

Thou wilt not leave us, wilt thou? look'st thou pale?
What says old Hunsdon? nay, I'll speak thy part:
Thy hand, old lord; I'm sure I have thy heart.
   Huns. Both hand and heart.

Enter the Third Post.

   Queen. Before thou speak'st, take that: if he be
      dead,
Our self will see his funeral honoured.
   3rd Post. I then proceed thus: when the great
      galleons
And galliasses had environ'd them,
The undaunted Frobisher, though round beset,
Cheer'd up his soldiers, and well mann'd his fights,
And standing barehead bravely on the deck,
When murdering shot, as thick as April's hail,
Sung by his ears, he wav'd his warlike sword,
Firing at once his tiers on either side
With such a fury that he brake their chains,
Shatter'd their decks, and made their stoutest ships
Like drunkards reel, and tumble side to side.
Thus, in war's spite and all the Spaniards' scoff,
He brought both ship and soldiers bravely off.
   Queen. War's spite, indeed; and we, to do him
      right,
Will call the ship he fought in the War's-spite.
Now, countrymen, shall our spirits here on land
Come short of theirs so much admir'd at sea?
If there be any here that harbour fear,
We give them liberty to leave the camp,
And thank them for their absence.
A march! lead on! we'll meet the worst can fall:
                  [*A march within.*
A maiden Queen is now your general.

As they march about the stage, Sir FRANCIS DRAKE *and*
Sir MARTIN FROBISHER *meet them, with Spanish*
ensigns in their hands, and drum and colours before
them.

   Queen. What mean those Spanish ensigns in the
      hands
Of English subjects?
   Drake. Gracious Queen,
They show that Spaniards' lives are in the hands
Of England's sovereign.
   Queen. England's God be praised !
But, prithee, Drake (for well I know thy name,
Nor will I be unmindful of thy worth)
Briefly rehearse the danger of the battle:
Till Frobisher was rescued we have heard.
   Drake. We then retir'd; and after council call'd,
We stuff'd eight empty hoys with pitch and oil,
And all the ingredients aptest to take fire,
And sent them where their proud Armada lay. .
The Spaniard, now at anchor, thought we had come
For parley, and so rode secure ; but when
They behold them flame like so many bright bonfires,
Making their fleet an Etna like themselves,
They cut their cables, let their anchors sink,
Burying at once more wealth within the sea,
Than th' Indies can in many years restore.
Now, their high built and large capacious bottoms
Being by this means unaccommodated,
Like to so many rough, unbridled steeds,
Command themselves, or rather are commanded
And hurried where th' inconstant winds shall please.
Some fell on quicksands, others brake on shelves :
Medina, their great grand and general,
We left unto the mercy of the sea ;

Don Pedro, their high admiral, we took,
With many knights and noblemen of Spain,
Who are by this time landed at St. Margaret's,
From whence your admiral brings them up by land,
And at St. James's means to greet your grace.

    Queen. Next under Heaven your valours have the
        praise!
But prithee, Drake, give us a brief relation of those ships,
That in this expedition were employ'd
Against the Spanish forces?

    Drake. The Elizabeth Jonas, Triumph, the White
        Bear,
The Mer Honora, and the Victory;
Ark Raleigh, Due Repulse, Garland, War's-spite,
The Mary Rose, the Bonaventure, Hope,
The Lion, Rainbow, Vanguard, Nonpareil,
Dreadnought, Defiance, Swiftsure, Anspach,
The Whale, the Scout, Achates, the Revenge.

    Queen. Drake, no more.—
Where'er this navy shall hereafter sail,
Oh, may it with no less success prevail!
Dismiss our camp, and tread a royal march
Toward St. James's, where in martial order
We'll meet and parley our Lord Admiral.
As for those ensigns, let them be safely kept,
And give commandment to the Dean of Paul's
He not forget, in his next learned sermon,
To celebrate this conquest at Paul's cross;
And to the audience in our name declare
Our thanks to Heaven, in universal prayer.
For though our enemies be overthrown,
'Tis by the hand of Heaven, and not our own.—
One sound a call.—Now, loving countrymen,   [*Call.*
And fellow soldiers, merited thanks to all.
We here dismiss you, and dissolve our camp.

Omnes. Long live, long reign our Queen Elizabeth!
Queen. Thanks, general thanks:
Towards London march we to a peaceful throne;
We wish no wars, yet we must guard our own.

[*Exeunt omnes.*

FINIS.

NOTES AND VARIOUS READINGS

TO THE SECOND PART OF

IF YOU KNOW NOT ME, YOU KNOW NOBODY.

Page 69, line 6, Actus Primus. Scæna Prima.]   This is the only mark
of an act or scene in the whole play, but the divisions are usually pretty
evident, from the course of the incidents, or from the progress of the dialogue.   In our notes, wherever it seemed at all necessary, we have pointed
out the changes of scenes; but, of course, the separation of the different
acts could only be a matter of conjecture, which, as heretofore, is left to
the reader.   We must suppose this first scene to occur in Gresham's ware-
house.

Page 70, line 28, Exit.]   The *exit* of the Barbary merchant is not
marked in the old copies.

Page 71, line 19, For twice the sum.]   "Meaning his cash," in the
margin of the old copies.

Page 71 line 34, London will yield you *partners* enow.]   In this line,
"partners" is to be read as a trisyllable; and such was formerly the case
with various words now used as dissyllables.

Page 72, line 3, You to *Portingal.*]   The common name of Portugal
at that date.

Page 72, line 22, *Ofter* than once or twice.]   *Oftener*, edit. 1632.

Page 73, line 11, A gown of a strumpet.]   *i.e., on* a strumpet.   Prepo-
sitions, in Heywood's time, and before and afterwards, were often used in
a way not employed in our day: Shakespeare affords innumerable instances.

Page 73, line 15, And [if] deeds of mercy, &c.]   Where words necessary to the sense of the author have been omitted in the old editions, we,
as usual, insert them between brackets.

Page 73, line 29, My morning exercise shall be at Saint Antlin's.]   "A
new morning prayer and lecture, the bells for which began to ring at five

in the morning, was established at St. Antholin's, in Budge Row, 'after Geneva fashion,' in September, 1559:" Cunningham's Handbook of London, 2nd edit., p. 15 : where see also other information as to the puritanical character of the preachings at St. Antolin's, or St. Anthony's.

Page 74, line 10, I'll beat *linen-bucks*.] Linen was of old carried to the wash in buck-baskets, and here by "linen-bucks" John Gresham seems to intend the linen that was contained in the bucks, and which was to be beaten in the water to make it clean. "This 'tis to have linen and buck-baskets."—"Merry Wives of Windsor," act iii., sc. 5.

Page 74, line 22, Now, afore God.] Now, *as I live*, edit. 1632.

Page 74, line 30, I'll give you leave to call me *cut*.] See this expression explained in a subsequent note to p. 90, line 28.

Page 74, line 33, Enter Hobson's 'Prentices, and a Boy.] The scene here changes to Hobson's shop.

Page 75, line 4, The Dagger, in Cheap.] The Dagger Tavern was in Cheapside; and hence, as appears afterwards, Dagger-pies, often mentioned by our old writers. In vol. ii. of "Extracts from the Stationers' Registers," p. 171, is mentioned the publication of " A fancie on the fall of the Dagger in Cheap," which may mean either that the house, or the sign which it bore, fell down: probably the latter, although the Editor, in his note on the entry, supposed that the word "fall" applied to the house. There was also a Dagger Tavern in Holborn : see Cunningham's Handbook of London, 2nd edit., p. 152.

Page 75, line 7, *Exeunt*.] The departure of the 'Prentices, leaving the shop to take care of itself, as Hobson found it, and their subsequent return, (both necessary stage-directions) are not mentioned in the old copies.

Page 75, line 19, And lay't not on their *jacks*.] A "jack" was originally used for a coat of mail, subsequently for a buff jerkin, and afterwards for nearly any kind of jacket worn by men and women. As early as Skelton's time, a "jack" meant an ordinary part of dress :—

> " So new facioned jackes,
> With brode flappes in the neckes,
> And so gay new partlettes
> Sawe I never."
>
> *Ballads*, printed for the Percy Society, 1840, p. 7.

Page 76, line 1, Your punks and *cockatrices*.] A cockatrice was the old cant name for a prostitute. See Ben Jonson's Works, by Gifford, ii., 9, (not 19, as given in the Index) and 39.

Page 76, line 7, Enter Pedlar *with* tawney coat.] *i.e.*, Enter a Pedlar *in a* tawney coat. The old copies print it, " Enter Pedlar, with Tawney-

coat," as if they were two persons, and the second speech is assigned to
Pedlar, and the fourth to Tawney-coat. They were the same person;
and it appears afterwards very clearly why the Pedlar is described as
wearing a *tawney coat.*

Page 76, line 26, As white as bears' teeth.] Possibly, these words apply
to the white money the Pedlar puts down, "to pay the old debt," before he contracts a new one.

Page 76, line 27, Bones a God, knaves!] Bones a *me*, knaves! edit.
1632.

Page 77, line 12, And 'tis thought yellow will grow a custom.] It did
so; and, in fact, it was so when Heywood wrote, as he informs us, though
the "custom" afterwards became almost universal. See "Dodsley's Old
Plays," last edit., vii., 132, &c.

Page 79, line 16, The *hot-houses* in Dieppe.] A "hot-house" was
then a very common name for a brothel.

Page 81, line 10, Enter Doctor Nowell, &c.] The scene here changes
to Lombard Street.

Page 81, line 16, Take you the *cause* in hand.] Take you the *course*
in hand, edit. 1632. Five lines lower, the same edition has "*their* persuasion" for "*fair* persuasion," the old and true reading.

Page 82, line 7, Enter Sir Thomas Ramsey.] In the old copies his
entrance is marked four lines earlier: possibly, he came in behind, while
Lady Ramsey and Dean Nowell were talking.

Page 84, line 19, *And* violent passions *do* sweep the soul, &c.] This
is the reading of edit. 1632, and it seems preferable to that of edit.
1606—

> " Why is't that force
> Are violent passions to sweep the soul," &c.

Page 85, line 35, Fore God, 'tis true.] *Indeed* 'tis true, edit. 1632.
We have not thought it necessary elsewhere to note variations of this
kind, occasioned by the greater strictness of the law subsequent to the
publication of edit. 1606.

Page 87, line 2, I'll have a *mansion* built.] So the later copies; but
the first reads—

> " I'll have a *roof* built, and such a roof," &c.

Page 87, line 29, Here, John, take this *seal* ring.] *Seal'd* ring, in the
old copies, both here and afterwards.

Page 88, line 17, Enter Timothy and John Gresham.] It is hardly
necessary to mention that the scene is here removed to Gresham's Ware-
house.

Page 88, line 24, I hope, John, you fear God.]   I hope, John, you fear *what you ought to fear*, edit. 1632.

Page 90, line 10, Yet proves a Judas often in his *payings*.]   Edit. 1606 has *dealings* for "payings" of the later copies.

Page 90, line 28, Let me be called *cut*.]   A term of contempt or abuse which has occurred before, p. 74, and is used by Shakespeare.   See "Twelfth Night," act ii., sc. 3, (Edit. Collier, iii., 359) where it is sufficiently explained, and its antiquity established.

Page 90, line 29, Enter Honesty, the Sergeant, and Quick.]   The scene here changes to a street, as is obvious from the course of the dialogue.

Page 91, line 17, The miching slave.]   "Miching" means *stealing*. See Shakespeare, edit. Collier, vii., 271, where it is also stated that "mallecho," in "Hamlet," is probably meant for the Spanish word *malhecho*— a suggestion recently made, in "Notes and Queries," as if it were a new discovery by the late Dr. Macginn.

Page 92, line 28, A trick to *catch* a fool.]   Edit. 1606 has, A trick to *chaste* a fool—clearly wrong.

Page 94, line 1, Enter Dr. Nowell, &c.]   In his own house, near St. Paul's, to which the scene is transferred.

Page 94, line 21, This was the picture, &c.]   In edit. 1606 only, this speech has no prefix.

Page 96, line 10, That freed *a beggar* at the grate of Ludgate.]   That freed *from begging* at the grate at Ludgate, edit. 1632, which, from the story, seems to be the true reading.   Stow, in his "Survey of London," 1599, p. 33, gives the name Stephen Forster.

Page 96, line 21, This, Ave Gibson, &c.]   Edit. 1606 has no prefix to this speech; and that of 1632 prints the name *Ann* Gibson.

Page 97, line 3, Although my children laugh, the poor may cry.].   So edit. 1606: but edit. 1632 gives the line thus:—

    "The poor may laugh, although my children cry;"
which may be the better reading.

Page 97, line 16, Than by *the* bad to wring.]   Edit. 1632 reads, perhaps preferably, "Than by *your* bad to wring."

Page 97, line 34, And take what they find.]   And take what they *can* find, edit. 1632.

Page 98, line 6, He is in huckster's handling.]   Edit. 1606 omits *He*, before this proverbial saying.

Page 100, line 34, Enter John Tawney-coat.]   The scene changes to a street into which Hobson's shop opens.   The Pedlar is still called John Tawney-coat, but he now wears a grey coat.

Page 101, line 1, Coming from the *Stocks.*] The Stocks, as it was called, stood on the ground now occupied by the Mansion House. (Cunningham's Handbook of London, p. 473, 2nd edit.) The signs of the houses mentioned by Tawney-coat form a curious note of locality: they were, no doubt, the very signs existing there in Heywood's time.

Page 101, line 19, At Bristow fair.] Bristol was then usually written and printed *Bristow.*

Page 103, line 2, Their master's hair grow through his *hood.*] Through his *head,* edit 1606.

Page 103, line 6, Do you hear, *hoiden?*] Gifford (Jonson's Works, vi., 171) says that hoiden is "confined to designate some romping *girl;*" but, in fact, it was applied to both sexes, and here we have it addressed to the Pedlar.

Page 103, line 12, Tell it out with a *wannion.*] *i.e.*, with a *vengeance,* of which one may possibly be a corruption of the other: the etymology of "wannion" is very doubtful.

Page 103, line 16, It appears he is beside himself.] It appears the poor fellow is besides himself, edit. 1632.

Page 104, line 18, As your city *Sumner.*] Or *Summoner.* In edit. 1606 it stands, "your city *Summer,*" which could hardly be right, unless it referred to Will Summer, or Summers, who had long been dead, having been jester to King Henry VIII: besides, he was anything but "known for a *knave,*" in the sense in which Tawney-coat uses the word.

Page 105, line 13, *Sit, good* John Tawney-coat.] *Welcome,* John Tawney-coat, edit. 1632.

Page 107, line 3, Or fetch a turn with[in] my upper walk.] The old copies have *with* for "within:" the change was required by the sense as well as by the measure.

Page 107, line 26, To any man will buy them, and remove them.] Stow (*Annales,* 1615, p. 1117) speaks as follows of this undertaking and its completion:—"Certain houses in Cornhill being first purchased by the citizens of London, at their charges, for certain thousands of pounds, were in the month of February cried by the Bellman, and afterwards sold to such persons as should take them down and carry them from thence; which was done in the months of April and May next following. And then, the ground being made plain, at the charges also of the city, (having cost them, one way and other, more than five thousand pound) possession thereof was by certain Aldermen, in the name of the whole citizens, given to the right worshipful Sir Thomas Gresham, knight, agent to the Queen's highness, there to build a place for merchants to assemble in, at his own proper charges; who on the seventh of June laid the first stone of the foundation, (being brick) and forthwith the workmen followed upon the same with such diligence, that by the month of November, in the year of our Lord 1567, the same was covered with slate. And on the 22 day of December, in the year of our Lord, 1568, the merchants of London left their meetings in Lombard Street, at such times as they had accustomed there to meet, and this day came into the new Burse, builded by Sir Thomas Gresham, as is afore showed."

Page 107, line 34, Of this, our *purchase.*]   So edit. 1606: edit. 1632 substitutes *purpose* for "purchase."

Page 109, line 1, In sooth, it will be a *good* edifice.]   Edit. 1632, a *goodly* edifice.

Page 109, line 8, And a *fair* space.]   And a *farre* space, edit. 1632.

Page 109, line 9, The round is *grated.*]   The old copies have *greater*, but we have ventured to alter it to *grated*, in conformity with what follows, where Sir T. Gresham explains the use of the "grates." *Greater* hardly makes sense of the passage.

Page 109, line 29, Here, like a *parish* for good citizens.]   Perhaps we ought to read *parvis* for "parish;" but the old copies are uniform.

Page 109, line 33, Shall come in trains to *pace* old Gresham's Burse.] To *trace* old Gresham's Burse, edit. 1632.

Page 109, line 35, And such a *globe* of beauty round about.]   *i.e.*, circle of beauty: Heywood was perhaps thinking of the Globe Theatre, which was circular.

Page 110, line 20, *A blazing star.*]   This blazing star, mentioned in the margin, may have easily been rendered visible to the audience by artificial means.

Page 111, line 14, Let's *live* to-day.]   So edit. 1632: edit. 1606 reads, Let's *have* to-day.

Page 111, line 23, The battle of Alcazar.]   The incidents relating to this battle had been brought upon the stage by George Peele, (at least, the play has in modern times been plausibly imputed to him) in a drama entitled "The Battle of Alcazar, fought in Barbary, between Sebastian, King of Portugal, and Abdelmelec, King of Morocco. With the death of Captain Stukeley," &c., 4to., 1594. See Peele's Works, edit. Dyce, ii., 82. A play in which Stukeley figured was performed by Henslowe's company in 1596: see Henslowe's Diary, p. 77. Whetstone, in his "English Myrror," 1586, p. 84, gives a narrative of the battle, but does not mention Stukeley.

Page 111, line 28, *Made* fellow with these kings.]   *Mad* fellow with these kings, edit. 1606—an epithet not undeserved by Stukeley.

Page 112, line 1, And the succeeding happy *heir*.] The necessary word "heir," omitted in edit. 1606, is from the later impressions.

Page 113, line 6, It may be the hangman will buy some of it for halters.] Hobson had sent for matches of goods, or pieces of similar pattern and fabric; and John Gresham had bought for him two thousand pounds' worth of such *match* as was of old used by soldiers for setting fire to gunpowder and other combustibles: it was made of tow, like rope.

Page 113, line 19, My *doubt* is more.] Possibly, "doubt" is misprinted for *debt;* but "doubt" is intelligible, and all the old copies concur in that word.

Page 114, line 27, The *pictures* graven of all the English kings.] By "pictures" was sometimes, of old, meant *statues*—perhaps, because statues were formerly often painted. This should be borne in mind in reading the last scene of "The Winter's Tale." The word "rooms," in the preceding line, means merely *places*, or niches.

Page 114, line 30, Admirable!] So edit. 1606; that of 1632 has, "Very admirable, and worthy praise."

Page 115, line 13, Leading in the Ambassador.] *i.e.*, the Russian Ambassador. In the next line, the old copies have, "the ambassadors set," which may refer to other ambassadors, accompanying the Russian Ambassador; but it seems more likely to be only a misprint. The scene, of course, here changes to the residence of Gresham.

Page 115, line 16, The *waits* in Sergeants' gowns.] The *waits* were the city musicians, and they were perhaps dressed "in Sergeants' gowns," for greater state. For with "*one* Interpreter," we should, perhaps, read, "with *an* Interpreter." The waits are again mentioned, on p. 135.

Page 115, line 22, And up.] These words, required by the metre, seem to have dropped out, in the first edition, and are adopted from later impressions.

Page 116, line 12, That ship's rich *freight*.] Edit. 1606 omits "freight."

Page 116, line 28, The several Ambassadors *there* will hear.] *Then* will hear, edit. 1606.

Page 117, line 24, And yet, *considering* all things.] And yet, *consider* all things, edit. 1606.

Page 117, line 33, Drawn in white marble.] Here we see that the "pictures" of the Kings and Queens of England, intended by Gresham for the "rooms" in his Burse, were not painted, but of white marble.

Page 118, line 32, This will *plague* him.] This will *plunge* him, edit. 1632.

Page 119, line 5, *Undo* my shoes.] *Unto* my shoes, edit. 1606.

Page 119, line 12, Cost *thirty thousand* pound.] *i.e.*, each slipper cost him £30,000. Six lines above, edit. 1606 has "thirty thousand" for "sixty thousand pound."

Page 119, line 27, Here *sixteen thousand pound* at one clap goes.] So the old copies, which we reprint; but the sum claimed by the jeweller (see p. 117) was only £1,500.

Page 119, line 34, As rich, as renowned, as any of all.] Edit. 1632 omits this line, and assigns the whole speech to Lady Ramsey.

Page 120, line 3, Thus treads on a king's present.] "Meaning the slippers," are explanatory words inserted in the margin.

Page 120, line 17, Enter Tawney-coat, with a *spade*.] With a *speed*, edit. 1606. Tawney-coat is the Pedlar, John Goodfellow, called, as we have seen, Tawney-coat from the dress he wears early in the play. He has been reduced to extreme poverty, and the scene here must be understood to represent the neighbourhood of Deptford, not very far from the Bankside. We must bear in mind that even the immediate vicinity of the Bankside, especially towards Newington Butts, was then all open fields and marshy grounds, much covered with wood, and not, as now, consisting merely of streets and houses.

Page 120, line 21, Than in the *flinty* bosoms of her children.] Than in the *flint-bosoms* of her children, edit. 1606.

Page 121, line 3, Whither wilt thou, wit?] A proverbial exclamation of frequent occurrence, and used by Shakespeare in "As You Like It:" see edit. Collier, iii., 76.

Page 121, line 15, Make them milk their *master* neighbour's kine.] Printed "their M. neighbour's kine," in the old copies.

Page 122, line 33, John *Goodfellow*, sir.] By an error of the transcriber, or printer, or by the forgetfulness of the poet, John Goodfellow, as Tawney-coat has been hitherto called, is here named John Rowland, in the old editions of this play. Of course, it has been necessary to observe consistency in this respect, and we have therefore changed Rowland to Goodfellow. Robin Goodfellow, the sprite, has been mentioned on the preceding page, and possibly the confusion has been occasioned by this circumstance.

Page 124, line 22, *You gravely* may better consider of that.] So edit. 1606; and it is so intelligible, that it is not necessary to substitute "*Your gravity* may consider of that," as in the edition of 1632.

Page 124, line 29, Yet I could say.] So edit. 1606: that of 1632 adds, "But I do not speak what I think, and yet I think more at this time than I mean to speak."

Page 125, line 7, As he, no question, does deserve.] Does deserve *something*, edit. 1632. Other minor variations, or corruptions, occur in this part of the scene.

Page 125, line 18, I'll raise thee, Goodfellow.] Here, again, we have been obliged to substitute Goodfellow for Rowland, but to the injury of the verse. Perhaps the name ought to have been Rowland throughout; but the manner in which Hobson's 'prentices sought for the name of John Goodfellow in their master's books, near the opening of the play, will not have been forgotten.

Page 125, line 26, Enter John and Courtesan.] The scene here shifts to France; and the license allowed to old dramatists, and the loud calls they made upon the imaginations of their auditors, are shown by the incident that Hobson first wanders to Deptford, and then proceeds to France in his nightcap, gown, and slippers, in order to detect John Gresham in his pranks.

Page 126, line 1, You'll ha' the first *veney*.] *Veney*, or *venie*, was a fencing term, from the French, and signified the touch or blow with the foil: " the first veney " is the first *hit*.

Page 126, line 13, Why, then, the Englishman for thy money.] This expression was proverbial, and a play was written by William Haughton, and printed in 1616, under the title of " Englishmen for my Money, or a Woman will have her Will." It was popular, and was republished in 1626 and 1631, the last time under the title of " A Woman will have her Will."

Page 128, line 1, Enter, at the other end of the stage, Hobson.] John and the Courtesan withdraw from one room into another, and, immediately, the stage is supposed to represent the outside of a house. Hobson knocks at a door, and is answered by *Puella*, (as she is called, in the stage-direction) probably from the balcony, which then was to be taken for a window.

Page 128, line 16, Here's an Englishman.] This speech is without the prefix " Wench," in edit. 1606.

Page 129, line 1, Enter John Gresham and Courtesan.] "Fact. Curtiz." is the imperfect stage-direction in the first edition; but the scene was rendered more intelligible afterwards. Still, in the then condition of the stage, it is not always easy to understand how this part of the play was managed, as regards the exits and entrances of the performers.

Page 129, line 8, *Intrat Puella*.] There seems no sufficient reason for putting these stage-directions in Latin; but, as they have been so given, in the old copies, and are not unintelligible, there seems no sufficient reason for altering them in our reprint.

Page 129, line 13, Do, my sweet Buffamache.] Buffalmaco is the name of a hero in Boccaccio, (Day viii., nov. 3) and he was brought upon the English stage by Marston; but why that name, or any corruption of it, should have been applied to this wench, may be doubted.

Page 130, line 6, Any man or woman to *occupy* for themselves.] So edit. 1606, but later impressions here (though not in the former instance) substitute *deal* for "occupy," and thus sacrifice a double meaning of the word, then well understood. Possibly, it was excluded by the Master of the Revels, in a very scrupulous humour, as in "Henry IV.," Part II., act ii., sc. 4. See Shakespeare, edit. Collier, iv., 384.

Page 130, line 17, A haberdasher of *small* wares.] John says, "of *all* wares," for the sake of his pretended excuse, and Hobson corrects him; but edit. 1632 has *all* in both places, by which the joke, such as it is, is sacrificed.

Page 131, line 13, Exit.] This necessary stage-direction is wanting in the first edition.

Page 131, line 31, *Intrat John, cum aliis Factoribus.*] Abridged in the old copies thus, *Intrat Joh. cum aliis fact.*

Page 132, line 11, *Measar mon a moy.*] This, and some of the gibberish that follows, could hardly be intended by Heywood for French, but merely for something that sounded like it. We print it as it stands in the original.

Page 132, line 30, Such as in the garden-alleys.] Such as *be* in the garden-alleys, in the later impressions; but the addition is not necessary.

Page 133, line 13, Hearty commendations.] John calls for "pen and ink," and here writes, and says aloud fragments of what he scribbles. It would have been more intelligible to have inserted *writes* in the margin, but the business of the scene seemed clear enough, without this interpolation.

Page 134, line 5, 'Tis logic to me, sir.] We are to imagine, here, that one of the Factors, pretended Frenchmen, jabbers something to Hobson, which he does not understand, and which he therefore says is logic to him.

Page 134, line 20, No more of French love, no more French loss shall do.] This is not very clear, and edit. 1632 substituted "No more of French, no more French craft shall do."

Page 134, line 22, Enter Sir Thomas Ramsey, &c.] After the preceding highly comic and well managed, though not very probable, scene, the stage now again represents part of the city of London. The first words of Sir Thomas Ramsey's speech afford another out of innumerable instances where "well *said*" is to be taken for well *done*.

Page 137, line 17, And whilst this voice flies through the *streets* forthright.] So edit. 1632: that of 1606 has *city* for "streets," to the injury of the metre, and no improvement of the passage, as, there is little doubt, the poet wrote it.

Page 137, line 26, Exeunt.] There is no notice of the departure of the Queen, her Courtiers, Citizens, &c., in edit. 1606. The true date of this royal opening of the Exchange was 23 January, 1570-1, and so it is given by Stow (*Annales*, 1615, p. 1131). It is unnecessary to quote the terms he employs, as Heywood closely follows them.

Page 137, line 27, Enter Dr. Nowell and Lady Ramsey.] The precise interval supposed to occur between this scene and the last is not known, as no authority that we have been able to consult gives the date of the last illness and death of Sir Thomas Ramsey. The stage now represents his house.

Page 138, line 12, A master of the Hospital.] *i.e.*, Christ's Hospital. Above, Tawney-coat is again called Rowland, instead of Goodfellow, his real name; at least, that he was first called by in this play. It does not suit the measure here so well as Rowland.

Page 139, line 4, Enter *Goodfellow, alias* Tawney-coat.] "Enter *Rowland, alias* Tawney-coat," old edits.

Page 141, line 7, Must not be *tardy*.] Printed *tarde*, and in italic, in the old copies, as if it were some strange word. It is singular how corruptions of the kind could be repeated in so many impressions. The place of action here is Greenwich.

Page 141, line 11, Whose virtue all the world——] A sentence, we may suppose, purposely left incomplete; but in some of the later editions the blank is filled up by, "Whose virtue *is unmatch'd.*"

Page 143, line 31, That I would do't for good of Catholics.] This line is omitted in edit. 1632. It will be remembered that vol. iii. of our Society's Papers contains the copy of an unique tract by Philip Stubbes, on the attempt of Dr. Parry to assassinate the Queen. Heywood follows the ordinary narratives.

Page 144, line 8, This man was *forwarder*, &c.] Edit. 1632 thus corrupts and spoils this and the next line:—

"This man was *forward* to thrust me forth,
Than now he is humble to accept *in me.*"

Page 144, line 23, *They retire*.] Not in the old copies, but necessary.

Page 145, line 8, Through any heavy want oppresseth thee.] Opposite these words, in the margin of edit. 1632, we read as follows:—"As she turns back, he offers to shoot, but, returning, he withdraws his hand."

Page 145, line 24, What doest thou with that *dag.*] A *dag* is a pistol, to which Parry referred, in the opening of his long soliloquy, p. 143. Respecting the word "dag," see "Dodsley's Old Plays," last edition, iii , 143; v., 302; ix., 188. It is needless to quote authorities. This incident, as our readers are aware, did not happen until many years after the Queen had christened the Royal Exchange.

Page 145, line 25, Pardon, thou villain, shows thou art a traitor.] Referring to the impunity the Queen had granted him for his attempt on the life of Hare, before mentioned. Edit. 1632 gives the line, " Pardon, thou villain, *that* shows thou art a traitor."

Page 146, line 11, *Arise.*] We doubt if this word were not meant for a stage-direction. We may conclude that Parry fell upon his knees, and that the Queen's speech ended with the close of the couplet.

Page 146, line 22, Enter John Gresham.] The scene is transferred to London. In the old copies, he is called " *Jack* Gresham," in the stage-direction, and " John " in the prefixes to his speeches.

Page 149, line 15, Do *my* poverty.] Edit. 1606 has, " Do *her* poverty."

Page 149, line 20, Till death us *depart.*] This is the old and true word in the marriage ceremony: in modern times, when the meaning of to " depart," as to *separate*, was forgotten, *do part* has been substituted for *depart.*

Page 151, line 2, And seems *mo* mild.] Some later impressions very needlessly alter "mo" to *more.*

Page 151, line 32, Enter Chorus.] The editions of this play, in 1606 and 1623, have no part of this Chorus, which is first found in edit. 1632. From that impression we have reprinted all the rest of this play, since it varies importantly from the earlier copies. The mode in which the drama imperfectly concludes in the first, and in some subsequent editions, may be seen at the close of our Introduction.

Page 152, line 16, Christopher *Carlisle.*] In the old copies, the name is misprinted *Carlake.*

Page 152, line 26, Enter the Duke of Medina, Don Pedro, &c.] This scene is on ship-board, in the Channel, as we find by the text.

Page 153, line 28, Climes that took up the greatest part o' th' *card.*] "Card" was then the ordinary term for *map :* hence, " to steer by the card ;" and, figuratively, " to talk by the card," in reference to exactness and safety of discourse.

Page 156, line 3, *Exeunt.*] The stage-direction, in the old copies, is *Exit*, and others perhaps went out with the Spaniard who brought the news that the English fleet had been descried.

Page 156, line 7, *Ballast* with the Pope's blessing.] *i.e.*, as we now say, *ballasted* with the Pope's blessing. So in the "Comedy of Errors," act ii., sc. 3, " Who sent whole armadoes of carracks to be *ballast* at her nose."

Page 156, line 13, Drum and colours. Enter the Earl of Leicester, &c.] The scene now becomes the famous camp near Tilbury; but we may be said to have no means of deciding how far the stage itself and its appurtenances accorded with these changes. Perhaps little more was done than what was effected by the appearance of the persons and their accoutrements, and the mention, very early in the dialogue, of the supposed place of action. "Drum and colours" may show that one drum and one pair of colours answered the purpose.

Page 161, line 16, *Sung* by his ears.] *Swung* by his ears, edit. 1632.

Page 161, line 25, Will call the ship he fought in the War's-spite.] A name, we believe, preserved in the British navy ever since.

THE END.

Also from Benediction Books ...

Wandering Between Two Worlds: Essays on Faith and Art
Anita Mathias
Benediction Books, 2007
152 pages
ISBN: 0955373700

Available from www.amazon.com, www.amazon.co.uk
www.wanderingbetweentwoworlds.com

In these wide-ranging lyrical essays, Anita Mathias writes, in lush, lovely prose, of her naughty Catholic childhood in Jamshedpur, India; her large, eccentric family in Mangalore, a sea-coast town converted by the Portuguese in the sixteenth century; her rebellion and atheism as a teenager in her Himalayan boarding school, run by German missionary nuns, St. Mary's Convent, Nainital; and her abrupt religious conversion after which she entered Mother Teresa's convent in Calcutta as a novice. Later rich, elegant essays explore the dualities of her life as a writer, mother, and Christian in the United States-- Domesticity and Art, Writing and Prayer, and the experience of being "an alien and stranger" as an immigrant in America, sensing the need for roots.

About the Author

Anita Mathias was born in India, has a B.A. and M.A. in English from Somerville College, Oxford University and an M.A. in Creative Writing from the Ohio State University. Her essays have been published in The Washington Post, The London Magazine, The Virginia Quarterly Review, Commonweal, Notre Dame Magazine, America, The Christian Century, Religion Online, The Southwest Review, Contemporary Literary Criticism, New Letters, The Journal, and two of HarperSanFrancisco's The Best Spiritual Writing anthologies. Her non-fiction has won fellowships from The National Endowment for the Arts; The Minnesota State Arts Board; The Jerome Foundation, The Vermont Studio Center; The Virginia Centre for the Creative Arts, and the First Prize for the Best General Interest Article from the Catholic Press Association of the United States and Canada. Anita has taught Creative Writing at the College of William and Mary, and now lives and writes in Oxford, England.

"Yesterday's Treasures for Today's Readers"
Titles by Benediction Classics available from Amazon.co.uk

Religio Medici, Hydriotaphia, Letter to a Friend, Thomas Browne

Pseudodoxia Epidemica: Or, Enquiries into Commonly Presumed Truths, Thomas Browne

Urne Buriall and The Garden of Cyrus, Thomas Browne

The Maid's Tragedy, Beaumont and Fletcher

The Custom of the Country, Beaumont and Fletcher

Philaster Or Love Lies a Bleeding, Beaumont and Fletcher

A Treatise of Fishing with an Angle, Dame Juliana Berners.

Pamphilia to Amphilanthus, Lady Mary Wroth

The Compleat Angler, Izaak Walton

The Magnetic Lady, Ben Jonson

Every Man Out of His Humour, Ben Jonson

The Masque of Blacknesse. The Masque of Beauty,. Ben Jonson

The Life of St. Thomas More, William Roper

Pendennis, William Makepeace Thackeray

Salmacis and Hermaphroditus attributed to Francis Beaumont

Friar Bacon and Friar Bungay Robert Greene

Holy Wisdom, Augustine Baker

The Jew of Malta and the Massacre at Paris, Christopher Marlowe

Tamburlaine the Great, Parts 1 & 2 AND Massacre at Paris, Christopher Marlowe

All Ovids Elegies, Lucans First Booke, Dido Queene of Carthage, Hero and Leander, Christopher Marlowe

The Titan, Theodore Dreiser

Scapegoats of the Empire: The true story of the Bushveldt Carbineers, George Witton

The Place of The Lion, Charles Williams

The Greater Trumps, Charles Williams

My Apprenticeship: Volumes I and II, Beatrice Webb

Last and First Men / Star Maker, Olaf Stapledon

Last and First Men, Olaf Stapledon

Darkness and the Light, Olaf Stapledon

The Worst Journey in the World, Apsley Cherry-Garrard

The Schoole of Abuse, Containing a Pleasaunt Invective Against Poets, Pipers, Plaiers, Iesters and Such Like Catepillers of the Commonwelth, Stephen Gosson

Russia in the Shadows, H. G. Wells

Wild Swans at Coole, W. B. Yeats

Five hundreth good pointes of husbandrie, Thomas Tusser

The Collected Works of Nathanael West: "The Day of the Locust", "The Dream Life of Balso Snell", "Miss Lonelyhearts", "A Cool Million", Nathanael West

Miss Lonelyhearts & The Day of the Locust, Nathaniel West

The Worst Journey in the World, Apsley Cherry-Garrard

Scott's Last Expedition, V1, R. F. Scott

The Dream of Gerontius, John Henry Newman

The Brother of Daphne, Dornford Yates

The Downfall of Robert Earl of Huntington, Anthony Munday

Clayhanger, Arnold Bennett

The Regent, A Five Towns Story Of Adventure In London , Arnold Bennett

The Card, A Story Of Adventure In The Five Towns , Arnold Bennett

South: The Story of Shackleton's Last Expedition 1914-1917, Sir Ernest Shackketon

Greene's Groatsworth of Wit: Bought With a Million of Repentance, Robert Greene

Beau Sabreur, Percival Christopher Wren

The Hekatompathia, or Passionate Centurie of Love, Thomas Watson

The Art of Rhetoric, Thomas Wilson

Stepping Heavenward, Elizabeth Prentiss

Barker's Delight, or The Art of Angling, Thomas Barker

The Napoleon of Notting Hill, G.K. Chesterton

The Douay-Rheims Bible (The Challoner Revision)

Endimion - The Man in the Moone, John Lyly

Gallathea and Midas, John Lyly,

Mother Bombie, John Lyly

Manners, Custom and Dress During the Middle Ages and During the Renaissance Period, Paul Lacroix

Obedience of a Christian Man, William Tyndale

St. Patrick for Ireland, James Shirley

The Wrongs of Woman; Or Maria/Memoirs of the Author of a Vindication of the Rights of Woman, Mary Wollstonecraft and William Godwin

De Adhaerendo Deo. Of Cleaving to God, Albertus Magnus

Obedience of a Christian Man, William Tyndale

A Trick to Catch the Old One, Thomas Middleton

The Phoenix, Thomas Middleton

A Yorkshire Tragedy, Thomas Middleton (attrib.)

The Princely Pleasures at Kenelworth Castle, George Gascoigne

The Fair Maid of the West. Part I and Part II. Thomas Heywood

Proserpina, Volume I and Volume II. Studies of Wayside Flowers, John Ruskin

Our Fathers Have Told Us. Part I. The Bible of Amiens. John Ruskin

The Poetry of Architecture: Or the Architecture of the Nations of Europe Considered in Its Association with Natural Scenery and National Character, John Ruskin

The Endeavour Journal of Sir Joseph Banks. Sir Joseph Banks

Christ Legends: And Other Stories, Selma Lagerlof; (trans. Velma Swanston Howard)

Chamber Music, James Joyce

Blurt, Master Constable, Thomas Middleton, Thomas Dekker

Since Yesterday, Frederick Lewis Allen

The Scholemaster: Or, Plaine and Perfite Way of Teachyng Children the Latin Tong , Roger Ascham

The Wonderful Year, 1603, Thomas Dekker

Waverley, Sir Walter Scott

Guy Mannering, Sir Walter Scott

Old Mortality, Sir Walter Scott

The Knight of Malta, John Fletcher

The Double Marriage, John Fletcher and Philip Massinger

Space Prison, Tom Godwin

The Home of the Blizzard Being the Story of the Australasian Antarctic Expedition, 1911-1914, Douglas Mawson

Wild-goose Chase , John Fletcher

If You Know Not Me, You Know Nobody. Part I and Part II, Thomas Heywood

The Ragged Trousered Philanthropists, Robert Tressell

The Island of Sheep, John Buchan

Eyes of the Woods, Joseph Altsheler

The Club of Queer Trades, G. K. Chesterton

The Financier, Theodore Dreiser

Something of Myself, Rudyard Kipling

Law of Freedom in a Platform, or True Magistracy Restored, Gerrard Winstanley

Damon and Pithias, Richard Edwards

Dido Queen of Carthage: And, The Massacre at Paris, Christopher Marlowe

Cocoa and Chocolate: Their History from Plantation to Consumer, Arthur Knapp

Lady of Pleasure, James Shirley

The Book of the Farm: - Detailing The Labours Of The Farmer, Steward, Plowman, Hedger, Cattle-Man, Shepherd, Field-Worker, and Dairymaid. (Volume I), Henry Stephens

The Book of the Farm: - Detailing The Labours Of The Farmer, Steward, Plowman, Hedger, Cattle-Man, Shepherd, Field-Worker, and Dairymaid. (Volume II), Henry Stephens

The Book of the Farm: - Detailing The Labours Of The Farmer, Steward, Plowman, Hedger, Cattle-Man, Shepherd, Field-Worker, and Dairymaid. (Volume III). by Henry Stephens

The Naturalist On The River Amazons, by Henry Walter Bates.

Antarctic Penguins: A Study of their Social Habits, Dr. George Murray Levick

The Dragon's Secret, Augusta Huiell Seaman.

The Nonsense Books: A Complete Collection of the Nonsense Books of Edward Lear, Edward Lear

The Cestus of Aglaia and The Queen of the Air With Other Papers and Lecture on Art and Literature, 1860-1870, John Ruskin.

The Last Days of Madrid: The End of the Second Spanish Republic, Segismundo Casado.

and many others…

Tell us what you would love to see in print again, at affordable prices! Email: **benedictionbooks@btinternet.com**